DÍLSEACHT

The story of Comdt. Gen. Tom Maguire and the Second (All-Ireland) Dáil

Ruairí Ó Brádaigh

First published in Ireland, April 1997 by
Irish Freedom Press
223 Parnell Street, Dublin 1, Ireland.

ISBN 0 9518567 8 2 (Hardback)

ISBN 0 9518567 9 0 (Paperback)

Media conversion, typesetting and book design by
Diskon Technical Services Ltd.
Cover Design by Níall Funge,
printed at the Elo Press Ltd., Dublin 8, Ireland,
and bound by PD Print Ltd., Dublin.

Commandant-General Thomas Maguire,
General Officer Commanding, Second Western Division,
Irish Republican Army, 1921.

In memory of my father and mother,
Matt Brady and May Caffrey
– Comrades of Tom Maguire in Donegal, Longford and Dublin –
who made me what I am.

Contents

Buíochas

All who assisted in any way in the preparation of this book are thanked, including the editor Seán Ó Brádaigh; the printer Paddy Funge; *SAOIRSE* for photographs; Dr Seán Maguire, Castlebar; Lita Ní Chathmhaoil, Baile Átha Cliath and Pat O'Brien, Roscommon agus Baile an Róba, Co. Mhaigh Eo.

The maps of the Tourmakeady Ambush are reproduced from *Raids and Rallies* by Ernie O'Malley, published by Anvil Books Ltd. The map of the IRA Divisional Areas 1921-23 is reproduced from *No Other Law* by Florence O'Donoghue, published by Anvil Books Ltd. Permission is gratefully acknowledged.

Réamhrá

I rish resistance to English aggression in which Tom Maguire played such a heroic part goes back over 800 years to the original Anglo-Norman invasion and colonisation of Ireland.

That resistance was maintained down the centuries. There was always a section of the Irish people who would not accept English domination and so the claim to separate Irish nationhood has been kept open and intact.

In the 1790s that resistance modernised itself by adopting the democratic Republican ideals of the American and French revolutions. The great national rising of 1798, brief flickerings in 1803 and 1848 and the Fenian Movement in Ireland and America were the continuation of the resistance. It emerged again in the 1916 Rising and the General Election of 1918 which led directly to the establishment of the First (All-Ireland) Dáil. Within a year of its foundation the 32-County Dáil was arbitrarily suppressed by the British government.

Against this background the young man named Tom Maguire in Mayo, already a member of the Irish Volunteers, and elated by news of the Rising in Dublin, determined to play a part in the unfolding struggle.

In the outcome what was as good as won in struggle was lost at the conference table. English Establishment guile and Irish weakness combined and a Treaty of Surrender was forced on Irish representatives in December 1921 under threat of "immediate and terrible war".

Ghéilleadar do cheann de "na trí rudaí is cóir a sheachaint: Gáire an tSasanaigh".

The Government of Ireland Act of the British parliament had sought to divide Ireland into Six and 26 Counties and succeeded in setting up a puppet partition parliament in Belfast. No Irish vote, unionist or nationalist, was cast for this measure.

The Treaty of 1921 addressed the failure of the Government of Ireland Act outside the North-East corner. The All-Ireland Republic already functioning throughout the country since 1919 was not to be recognised. It was to be suppressed in favour of a 26-County Dominion within the British Empire to be known as the Irish Free State.

Dílseacht

The Irish word Dílseacht is a most appropriate title for this book dedicated to the life and work of General Tom Maguire. It means fidelity, loyalty, sincerity, love.

The adjective dílis is used in such terms as an t-oidhre dílis, the lawful heir; and an rí dílis, the lawful sovereign, as opposed to the usurper.

Tom Maguire belonged to the Dáil dílis of all 32 Counties and therefore to the Rialtas dílis, the lawful Government of Ireland.

All members of the parliament of the new Free State would be required to swear allegiance to the King of England; the British Forces would maintain naval bases in the 26 Counties and the exorbitant Land Annuities would be paid over to the British Treasury.

Most important of all, the Belfast puppet parliament would control the six north-eastern counties of Antrim, Down, Armagh, Derry, Tyrone and Fermanagh. A Boundary Commission was promised to place the new Border "in accordance with the wishes of the inhabitants". This in time proved to be yet another empty English ruling-class promise made to beguile the Irish representatives.

The Belfast junta increased their Special Constabulary militia to 50,000, armed and paid by the British government. With the support of 13 battalions of British troops they ruthlessly seized control of the entire Six-County area.

County Councils in Tyrone and Fermanagh and other local bodies which gave allegiance to the All-Ireland Dáil were immediately suppressed by brute force and their officials physically removed from office.

When Republican resistance to the Great Betrayal in both Six and 26 Counties had been defeated by British arms and money, the Boundary Commission met at last but the Border was re-affirmed as in the Government of Ireland Act, and the Six-County and 26-County statelets were confirmed.

The "carrot" which bought certain Irish acquiescence in the Treaty of Surrender proved worthless. By 1925 the Irish struggle was of course totally demobilised and English Establishment treachery had triumphed, safe – for the moment – from Irish resistance.

In the dramatic events of these years, and later, the man whose story is told in these pages played a central role, as an Irish military commander in the field and as an elected Deputy in the revolutionary parliament created by the self-determination of the whole Irish people, acting as a unit. His story is that of Ireland's struggle for national freedom and independence throughout most of the twentieth century. It is an extremely interesting tale.

Guerilla Leader
and Teachta, Dáil Éireann

WHEN COMDT-GENERAL Tom Maguire of Cross, Co Mayo died on July 5, 1993 he was not alone the last general officer of the Irish Republican Army of 1921, but also the last and faithful survivor of the Second (All-Ireland) Dáil elected in the same year. General Maguire had reached the great age of 101 years and was Patron of Republican Sinn Féin since 1987. He had served the All-Ireland Republic for 80 years of his life and the outstanding characteristic of his career, in both its military and political aspects was his dílseacht, his unswerving fidelity to that Republic.

Tom Maguire tells his own story – his background and his involvement with the Republican Movement up to 1955 in a twenty-five page interview related to Uinseann Mac Eoin and carried in the book *Survivors* (published 1980 and 1987). Here we have his own account, in his own words and from his own lips, of his participation in the great revolutionary events of the first half of the twentieth century in Ireland.

Maguire's style in his account of the South Mayo Brigade Column's action against British forces at Tourmakeady in 1921 is described as a report which "for modesty and understatement can rank with anything that Caesar ever wrote in his commentary on his wars in Gaul".[1]

This must be borne in mind when reading the interview with him.

VÉARSA AS LOCH MEASCA

Ag dul trí Thuar Mhic Éadaigh dom
Sea thosaigh mé ag smaoineamh,
Ar an té a sheas fód le Dúchrónaigh
I mbliain naoi déag fiche a haon.
Fágaim slán is beannacht dóibh,
Flaitheas Dé go dtugtar dóibh,
Ar thit at thaobh Loch measca
Atá suite i measc na sliabh.

– Sliocht as dán le Tomás Ó Donnchadha

Tom Maguire joined the Irish Volunteers shortly after they were founded in 1913. He was "well aware of the issues" when Redmond split them with his recruiting speech for the British army in 1914. Consequently there were only a few Irish Volunteers in his area when 1916 came and they could play no part, unlike the Galway men and women under Liam Mellows.

The Easter Rising came on them "like a bolt from the blue". He would never forget his exhilaration and it became a

SINSIR THOMÁIS MHIG UIDHIR

Sa bhliain 1691 tháinig Cúchonnacht Mag Uidhir aduaidh ó Fhear Manach le buíon fear chun troid ar son cearta Gael ag Eachroim, Co na Gaillimhe. Maraíodh ann é. Scaipeadh a lucht leanúna, sinsir Thomáis Mhig Uidhir ina measc.

Bhuail siad siar trasna Co na Gaillimhe de réir a chéile agus chuir siad fúthu in Áth Cinn, agus sa Chrois, Co Mhaigh Eo ina dhiaidh sin.

Bhí Liam Mharcuis Mag Uidhir in éineacht le Seoirse de Bláca as Gearrachluain ag fáiltiú roimh an nGinearál Humbert agus a chuid saighdiúirí a tháinig ón bhFrainc i 1798. Bhí Liam sa chath ag Béal Átha na Muc, Co Longfoirt. Bhí muscaed leis ag athair Thomáis ach cailleadh é aimsir na nDúchrónach.

Chaith an Fínín, Séamas Mac Stiofáin seal gearr i dteach sheanathar Thomáis. Bhí athair Thomáis, Liam Mag Uidhir agus a dheartháir Pádraic páirteach i gCogadh na Talún agus bhí siad i láthair ag an gcruinniú mór sa Bhaile Gaelach, Co Mhaigh Eo. Ba é Liam a ghlaoigh amach na fir oibre a bhí ag obair don Chaptaen Boycott.

Ní haon ionadh mar sin go raibh an náisiúnachas i bhféitheacha Thomáis.

turning point in his life, as with so many other Irish people. "To think that Irishmen were fighting England on the streets of Dublin: I thanked God for seeing such a day."

The first properly organised company of the IRA in the Cross area of Co. Mayo was formed in 1917, but they had no arms. Tom coveted the eight rifles in the hands of the Royal Irish Constabulary in the local barracks – "they were trained as a military force, very much like the RUC today". They were "an extension of the British army except that they wore different uniforms". Those that remained in the RIC were "terribly bitter towards the end, far tougher fighters to have to deal with than the soldiers".

Tom Maguire tells of his attempts to capture the RIC rifles and when the Mayo Brigade of the IRA was divided in four in September 1920, he was appointed OC of the South Mayo Brigade. There was much land agitation and agrarian trouble locally that year and the Volunteers tried repeatedly to ambush the enemy.

Meanwhile Tom had become a member of the Irish Republican Brotherhood as re-organised after 1916. The IRB oath was administered to him by the Adjutant of the County Mayo Brigade, Dick Walsh of Claremorris who was Maguire's superior officer earlier in the year. The IRB membership was a significant development as shall be seen.

Eventually the South Mayo Brigade Flying Column succeeded in making contact. They ambushed a lorry-borne

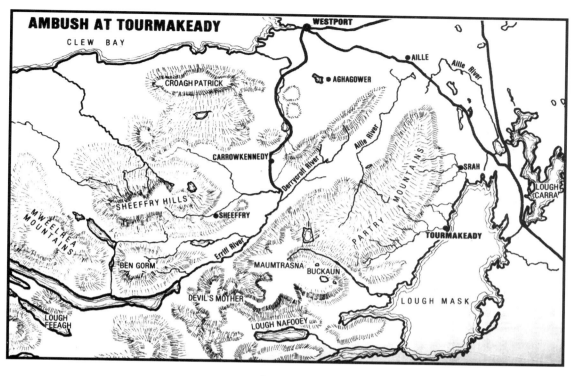

AMBUSH AT TOURMAKEADY

CLEW BAY

WESTPORT

AILLE

Aille River

AGHAGOWER

CROAGH PATRICK

Aille River

CARROWKENNEDY

Derrycraff River

SRAH

LOUGH CARRA

P A R T R Y   M O U N T A I N S

SHEEFFRY HILLS

SHEEFFRY

M W E E L R E A   M O U N T A I N S

Erriff River

TOURMAKEADY

BEN GORM

MAUMTRASNA

BUCKAUN

DEVIL'S MOTHER

LOUGH MASK

LOUGH FEEAGH

LOUGH NAFOOEY

party of British troops in open country at a place called Kilfall on the road between Ballinrobe and Castlebar on March 7, 1921. Four soldiers fled, one was wounded and the rest surrendered to Volunteers armed with shotguns using buckshot. Six to eight service rifles were now in their possession.

On May 3 came surely the greatest operation of the Black-and-Tan War in the West of Ireland when "Thirty IRA men defied 600 British troops at Tourmakeady".[2] The RIC had been withdrawn from smaller barracks such as Cross, Cong, Clonbur, Partry and Ballyglass. At Derrypark or more correctly Ceapach na Creiche the enemy maintained a garrison of twelve, stiffened in fighting and aggressive strengths by Black-and-Tans.

The plan was to ambush the convoy bearing pay and provisions that went out to this barracks from Ballinrobe once a month in the Gaeltacht village of Tourmakeady on the western shore of Lough Mask. Ernie O'Malley says in *Raids and Rallies*, p 117 that "the uncertainty that existed among the constabulary in small posts in remote districts helped to wear down their nerves. In many places they were

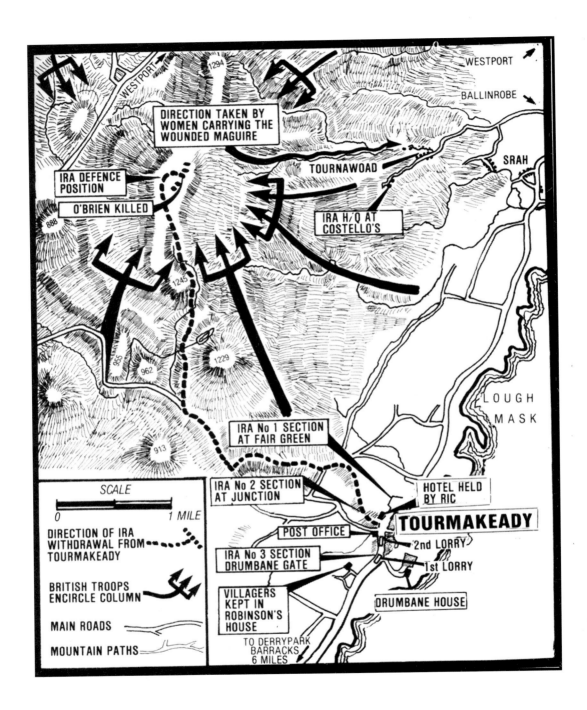

SCALE

0   1 MILE

DIRECTION OF IRA
WITHDRAWAL FROM
TOURMAKEADY

BRITISH TROOPS
ENCIRCLE COLUMN

MAIN ROADS

MOUNTAIN PATHS

WESTPORT

BALLINROBE

SRAH

DIRECTION TAKEN BY
WOMEN CARRYING THE
WOUNDED MAGUIRE

TOURNAWOAD

IRA DEFENCE
POSITION

O'BRIEN KILLED

IRA H/Q AT
COSTELLO'S

LOUGH
MASK

IRA No 1 SECTION
AT FAIR GREEN

IRA No 2 SECTION
AT JUNCTION

HOTEL HELD
BY RIC

POST OFFICE

TOURMAKEADY

2nd LORRY

IRA No 3 SECTION
DRUMBANE GATE

1st LORRY

VILLAGERS
KEPT IN
ROBINSON'S
HOUSE

DRUMBANE HOUSE

TO DERRYPARK
BARRACKS
6 MILES

an outpost beleaguered more by the withdrawal of the surrounding people and the menace of the encircling hills than by the threat of IRA efficiency".

When the Crown Forces placed their order for provisions in Birmingham's shop in Ballinrobe, a Volunteer named Patrick Vahey who worked there got the message through to the Column lying in wait at Tourmakeady. Maguire notes that "in later years (Patrick Vahey) would have been an uncle of Frank Stagg who died – many say he was killed – suffering intolerable conditions in English prisons in February 1976".

Another Volunteer named Pádraic Feeney of Ballinrobe also attempted to bring information to the Brigadier. He set out by bicycle but saw the military escort pass him on the way. He continued on hoping to join the fight but was taken prisoner by the RIC and held in a local hotel where some of them barricaded themselves during the ambush. Later they took him out the back and shot him dead. Pádraic Feeney's sister Christina was later to marry Tom Maguire (in December 1924 when he was still on the run).

Five of the enemy were killed in the ambush – the shotguns doing their deadly work – and more were wounded. The IRA suffered no casualties and withdrew to the nearby Partry mountains while the RIC at Derrypark sent word to Ballinrobe by wireless transmitter that the convoy had been attacked. The mountains were bare and offered little cover as Column Commander Maguire surveyed the surrounding countryside using his field glasses.

He counted twenty-four dust clouds as enemy reinforcements in lorries made for Tourmakeady from Galway, a brigade headquarters, and from Claremorris, Tuam and Ballinrobe. Other reinforcements of RIC and British troops converged on the area from Westport and Castlebar. The column was being steadily surrounded as the lorries halted and concentrated Lewis gun and rifle fire on their position.

A pitched battle took place on the hillside with the Column Commander's arm being fractured by a burst from a Lewis gun. As his Adjutant, Michael J. O'Brien, attended to his Commander's wounds a British officer shot him dead. An enemy assault party had made their way forward unobserved by the Column men who were pinned down by intense British fire. The officer was in turn wounded and he and his party retreated.

From 4 p.m. till darkness at 10.30 in hunger and thirst

South Mayo Brigade IRA Flying Column, 1921

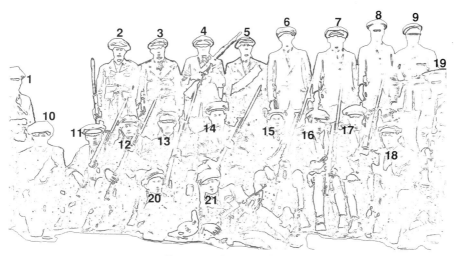

SOUTH MAYO BRIGADE

1.	Tom Maguire (Commandant)	12.	Séamus Burke
2.	Martin Flannery	13.	Michael Shaughnessy
3.	Unknown	14.	Michael Corliss
4.	Unknown	15.	Michael O'Brien
5.	Jim Duffy	16.	Tom Carney
6.	Unknown	17.	Patrick Gibbons
7.	Terry O'Brien	18.	? Murphy
8.	John Collins	19.	Paddy Maye
9.	Tom Lally	20.	Michael Costello
10.	John McGing	21.	John Ferguson
11.	Tom Cavanaugh		

the Column men clung tenaciously to the mountainside returning fire sparingly with their diminishing ammunition. When the enemy withdrew leaving a skeleton force which fired Verey lights at intervals, they passed through the encircling lines, their Adjutant dead and their Commander hit six times. Tom Maguire was carried to safety from the mountainside; in subsequent days he had many hair-breadth escapes and his recovery was slow and tedious.

Fresh troops with spotter airplanes combed the area for four days but to no avail. Men of the Newport and Westport Columns of the West Mayo Brigade under Michael Kilroy arrived to relieve the pressure only to find that the South Mayo Column had escaped.

The British suffered ten killed and seven wounded that day with six others being hit; the IRA lost their Brigade Adjutant and Vol Feeney and another Volunteer was slightly wounded. Ten shotguns were lost, but four rifles, three revolvers with rifle and revolver ammunition were captured. The Column Commander spent the four days within the cordon, housed by night and concealed by bracken by day.

The Crown garrisons at Derrypark, Kinnury and Cuilmore were immediately withdrawn for their own safety. Ernie O'Malley sums up: "The enemy had to use additional men for patrols and for convoys and this increase, when multiplied by the demand for more troops in other centres of unease throughout the country, fixed the strain on imperial defence at too tense a breaking point".

"In this way," he concludes, "a minor operation contributed to the sum total of influence which made it impossible for the British to rule the country by force. Lloyd George was forced to admit in the British House of Commons that 'the King's Writ no longer runs in Ireland'."

After Tourmakeady the Maguire home at Cross was destroyed by British troops and police "on punitive raids as they call them now in the North" (Tom's own words). Three times local people put out fires they started inside. Then the Crown Forces demolished it completely. It had to be rebuilt after the 1922-23 conflict; with the family coach-building business in ruins this was not an easy task.

Later, on May 19, 1921 Tom Maguire was elected to the Second (All-Ireland) Dáil Éireann with three other Sinn Féin TDs for the constituency of South Mayo-South Roscommon. It was to be a fateful occurrence.

Still not fully restored to health he attended the first meeting of the new Dáil in August when De Valera was confirmed in his appointment as President of the Republic. The Truce in July had come as a "bombshell" to Maguire whose first thought was that "the English are after this so we must have won".

With intensified training during the Truce period, the divisionalising of the Republican Army continued. North Galway, South Mayo and South Roscommon Brigades with the Ballyhaunis Battalion from East Mayo were grouped together as the Second Western Division. Tom Maguire was appointed General Officer Commanding, holding the rank of Commandant-General with authority under a commission signed by Cathal Brugha, the All-Ireland Minister for Defence. Tom treasured that commission until the day of his death.

Treaty suppresses the Republic

ON DECEMBER 6, 1921 the Treaty of Surrender was signed in London under duress. British Premier Lloyd George had threatened "immediate and terrible war". Tom Maguire says: "I was overwhelmed when the news came through that a Treaty such as this one had been signed. I was absolutely convinced that the Republic that the people had established had to be recognised."

He continued: "I did not see the North as a separate issue. What counted was that the vast majority of the people of Ireland had voted for a Republic and we had no right to disestablish it."

Earlier he had said: "When the terms of the Treaty were published, six months later (post-Truce), I said 'How could Irishmen have put their names to it?'" Asked if those who signed it should have been arrested on their return, he said "No". He blamed De Valera who had the responsibility as President of the Republic, publicly re-elected to "formally record our status as a Republic in view of the negotiations then commencing".

"Yet the treaty they were engaged in negotiating was designed to subvert the Republic. He was in a very strong position had he wished to press it. He had the Army overwhelmingly behind him. He should therefore have acted decisively when they came back; he should not have allowed a vote. He should simply have said, we cannot do this, and he would have had the support of the nation."

In plain words, Maguire held that to approve of the Treaty of Surrender was *ultra vires*, beyond the power of the Cabinet or the Dáil; it was unconstitutional and De Valera should not have permitted it to be voted on since neither Cabinet nor Dáil had the authority to subvert or overthrow themselves.

On a personal note, Tom Maguire had "the greatest respect for Mulcahy (IRA Chief-of-Staff) whom I met a number of times... He had none of the Mick Collins bonhomie. He was very much the leader and a disciplinarian. In fact I liked him very much because he was so straight and forthright. I had met Mick Collins also (Director of Intelligence, Minister for Finance and Head of the IRB)".

"I thought he was very solid, but I did not like his habit of taking the country fellows off for a jar. He got a grip on fellows that way, but Mulcahy would not do that; he was all business. Still all of us had faith in Mick, yet they undermined him also. Some blame the IRB for this, with good reason".

Tom went to Dublin on December 13 for the Dáil debate on the Treaty (or the Surrender as he saw it, both political and military). He was met in the hallway of his hotel, the Exchange in Parliament Street, by his senior in the IRB, Mícheál Ó Droighneáin, as na Forbacha, who was attached to the East Connemara Brigade. His message was that senior officers in the IRB supported the Treaty. It is presumed that all Deputies who were IRB members were similarly pressured.

If there was a significant pressure within the Movement there were powerful forces acting outside it also. There was no radio or television then but the press was unanimously, relentlessly and ruthlessly pro-Surrender. Of all the dailies, evening papers and local weeklies, one and only one – *The Connaughtman* published in Sligo – was for the Republic.

The Catholic Hierarchy supported Lloyd George's ultimatum with vigour. Tom tells how his parish priest Canon Hennelly wrote to him: "If you cannot see your way to vote for it you should at least abstain". Dean Dalton of Ballinrobe ordered him to vote for the Treaty. That was offensive, in Tom's opinion, and he did not reply. Even the Chinese Mission at Dalgan Park near Shrule, Co Mayo wrote. Tom replied to these setting out his reasons clearly. Canon Hennelly answered saying his Archbishop had asked him "to use all my influence".

"The pressure was strong and concerted on every TD and those who returned home over Christmas were the most exposed. It has been said with truth that if the vote had been taken before Christmas it would not have been carried." Tom had a bad bout of influenza and stayed in Dublin. He tells how after the holiday Dean Dalton and the parish priest of Kilmaine wished to see him at the Gresham Hotel. In high good humour they ordered champagne. Tom had a brown ginger.

He spoke just two words in the debate at Earlsfort Terrace. "Ní toil". (I do not agree).[3] When the vote was taken on January 7, one other Deputy said to him, "If I had known that you were going to vote against it, I would have

BETRAYING THE REPUBLIC IN THE NAME OF THE REPUBLIC

Griffith was elected President of Dáil Éireann (the Government of the Irish Republic) on January 10, 1922. Two days later in his capacity as Chairman of the Delegation to London which signed the Treaty he summoned a meeting of the "Parliament of Southern Ireland" for January 14. This was a partitionist body for 26 Counties only created by the British Government of Ireland Act of 1920 and rejected by the people in May 1921 when they elected their Deputies to the All-Ireland Dáil.

Griffith was Head of Dáil Éireann and yet he called into existence a rival parliament — surely an action without precedent in history. Likewise Mulcahy in the very last words spoken in the Dáil on January 10 said: "It is suggested that I avoided saying the Army will continue to be the Army of the Irish Republic. If any assurance is required — the Army will remain the Army of the Irish Republic." (applause)

In the name of the Republic was the Republic betrayed...

Earlier that day Griffith had said: "The Republic of Ireland remains in being until the Free State comes into being... Whatever position the President (de Valera) occupied, if I am elected I will occupy the same until the people have the opportunity of deciding for themselves... If I am elected I will keep the Republic in being until after the Free State is established when the people can decide for and against... I want the Republic kept in being until the people can have a free election and give their votes."

These were express undertakings to maintain the Republic, yet these men's subsequent actions totally belied their words.

voted against it too." This showed how casually, in Tom's opinion, it was approved with a majority of only seven, 64 to 57.

Both Ernie O'Malley[4] and Brian O'Higgins[5] say only three supported it on its merits. The remaining 61 did so as the only alternative to war or as "a stepping-stone to the Republic". De Valera and his Cabinet resigned and when Griffith succeeded him two days later it was by two votes only, 60 to 58.

Mulcahy replaced Cathal Brugha as Minister for Defence and stated: "The Army will remain occupying the same position with regard to this Government of the Republic, and occupying the same position with regard to the Minister of Defence, and under the same management, and in the same spirit as we have had up to the present." (Dáil Éireann: Debate on the Treaty, p 428, January 10, 1922).

Men like Tom Maguire knew this was nonsense. The new Cabinet was pledged under the Treaty to destroy the Republic and that they proceeded to do. On January 14 the

"Parliament of Southern Ireland" met, attended by 60 pro-Treaty and four Unionist Deputies from Trinity College. They passed the Treaty and set up a "Provisional Government" to implement it, with Michael Collins as Chairman.

To safeguard the Republic the majority of IRA Divisional Commandants met with the minority of the GHQ Staff who stood by the Republic and formed a Military Council. On January 11, Tom Maguire's name was among the signatories of a letter to Mulcahy demanding an Army Convention immediately. If this were denied they would set up an independent Headquarters Staff themselves.

Ernie O'Malley[6] describes Tom at that first meeting: "Tom Maguire was quiet looking. He spoke in monosyllables, nodded often instead of replying. He had been a farmer although he did not look like a farmer. (Not so, he was a coachbuilder. – Ed) He might have been a teacher in a college."

The British supplied arms and munitions to the pro-Treaty section or Free State army who were ceded Dublin Castle and Beggar's Bush Barracks. They dealt with the new 26-County "Provisional Government" and not with the Dáil – even with its Free State Cabinet. Churchill, British Colonial Secretary, made it clear: "We have never recognised Dáil Éireann and we never shall." The All-Ireland Dáil was a revolutionary body and it was being steadily undermined and replaced.

Mulcahy tried bargaining, then agreed to the Army Convention on March 26, then on St Patrick's Day had it banned because he foresaw an adverse decision for the Treaty position. The Ard-Fheis of Sinn Féin met in February and while the feeling was strongly anti-Treaty, adjourned for three months. Thus the Army had to face up to a decision the political wing of the Movement had side-stepped.

The proclaimed Convention met as arranged in the Mansion House, Dublin with 75 to 80% of delegates attending. They withdrew allegiance from the Dáil which they believed had betrayed the Republic. Henceforth they would be loyal only to their own Executive which the Convention elected. Tom Maguire was opposed to the withdrawal of allegiance; he felt it was a mistake but he was elected to the new Army Executive which appointed a new Headquarters Staff.

The Convention adjourned and resumed on April 9. Maguire did not continue on the Executive and suggested Michael Kilroy, GOC Fourth Western Division to replace him. This was accepted. Later, O'Malley as Director of Organisation on the new GHQ toured the West: "I saw Tom Maguire in Ballinrobe near the lake country, after I had visited rock-swept Connemara." Tom had established his Divisional Headquarters in the evacuated British infantry barracks, now in ruins behind the present 26-County police barracks.

Earlier in March, a massive, dramatic confrontation took place in Limerick city when Free State elements from Clare were ordered by Mulcahy into the Second Southern Division area in an attempt to seize barracks being vacated by the British. Ernie O'Malley as Divisional GOC summoned assistance from the three Western Divisions and Tom Maguire with a contingent of his Volunteers arrived by train. The Free Staters had to back down and the city was left in the hands of the local Mid-Limerick Brigade, IRA.

In April, clashes, with the loss of at least six lives, took place in Leinster as the Free State extended and tightened its grip. They consolidated their position in Mullingar, ejected the Republican Volunteers from Athlone Barracks and in early May captured Kilkenny after a siege of the ancient Ormond castle.

With the situation deteriorating rapidly an Electoral Pact was reached between De Valera and Collins for an agreed election and a Coalition Government. The resumed Ard-Fheis of Sinn Féin passed it unanimously and the 32-County Dáil ratified it. Collins was actively assisting IRA units North of the Border and promised a Republican Constitution. He was called to London and on his return to Cork on June 14th, two days before the election, publicly broke the Pact. The Constitution published on Polling Day was shamelessly Free State.

The effect of this agreement was that sitting TDs in 26-County constituencies would be returned unopposed by either Free State or Republican candidates but other interests would be free to contest. Tom Maguire, Harry Boland and two pro-Treaty Deputies were elected in South-Mayo-South Roscommon.

Tom had welcomed the Pact but felt it gave a "residual advantage" to the Free State parties. He believed that in the

West, the South and most of Dublin the Free Staters would have been routed. "The Pact tied our hands," he said, "and guaranteed them seats." True, the Second, Third and Fourth Western Divisions were solidly Republican, as were the First and Second Southern and the Dublin and South Dublin Brigades. In the outcome 94 Pact candidates were returned, 58 pro-Treaty and 36 Republicans out of a total of 128.

The Third (All-Ireland) Dáil was to meet on June 30 but the Free Staters under public and private pressure from London pre-empted the situation and attacked the Republican Headquarters in Dublin's Four Courts with artillery given by the British. The Dáil did not meet; Tom Maguire did not go to Dublin for its sitting but "stood to" at his Divisional HQ in Ballinrobe. He knew that the shelling of the Four Courts had opened the decisive stage of the counter-revolution.

POSITION OF SIX-COUNTY DEPUTIES UNDER THE COLLINS-DE VALERA PACT

The Second Dáil, on May 20, 1922 approved the "National Coalition Panel Joint Statement" signed by de Valera and Collins. Point 5 of that agreement read: "That the constituencies where an election is not held shall continue to be represented by their present Deputies." An election was then decreed for June 16 for 28 listed constituencies which taken together made up 26 Counties.

Those where no election was decreed – the Dáil did not control the election machinery there – added up to the Six Counties. Of the six Deputies elected to the Dáil from these constituencies in 1921 five were also returned for constituencies in the 26 Counties. Four of these were pro-Treaty, leaving the Republicans with de Valera representing Down and Seán O'Mahony for Fermanagh-Tyrone.

Since de Valera also represented Clare, O'Mahony was the sole Deputy from the Six Counties who did not have to seek re-election in 1922. The last meeting of the Second (All-Ireland) Dáil, before the pro-Treaty element withdrew, was held on June 8. The last line of the Official Report of the Dáil (p 513) states: "The House then adjourned to Friday, 30th June, 1922."

THE DEFENCE OF THE REPUBLIC

IN HIS CAPACITY as GOC Second Western Division IRA, Comdt-General Maguire issued a manifesto on July 4 which was published in the *Connacht Telegraph*, Castlebar on July 8. Headed "Óglaigh na hÉireann – Fógradh" it speaks of "an unprovoked attack... on the Headquarters of our army in Dublin" by Provisional Government forces. A similar attack could be made on the Second Western and they wished to make it known to the citizens resident in their area that "we have no desire to make war on any section of the Irish people".

The policy from 1913 had been to protect the people from foreign aggression. Since the Declaration of Independence issued by the First Dáil in 1919, they had fought to maintain the Republic then established. They now deemed it their duty to resist the attempt to subvert that Republic and to prevent the achievement of "that which the British Imperial Army failed to achieve".

"The Free State forces," it went on, "are being armed and equipped by the British Government. We, on the other hand, are regarded as the enemies of England and we must depend solely on ourselves and on the people of Ireland. We are absolutely confident that, having Right and Principle on our side, and having as our comrades men who will rather die than surrender our unquestionable right to absolute independence, we shall win and that the People will stand by us in our fight for Freedom."

In July and August, no parliament, Republican or Free State met in Dublin. When Count Plunkett applied in the Supreme Court of the Republic during July for a writ of habeas corpus for the liberation from prison of his son George, who had been arrested by the Free State, the Republican Courts were suppressed. (Churchill had promised this in the British House of Commons earlier that day).

In August, Deputy Kathleen Clarke (widow of the 1916 leader) applied to the Supreme Court for a *mandamus* to be directed to Eoin MacNeill as Ceann Comhairle commanding him to summon the final meeting of the Second Dáil which had not taken place on June 30. It could then

ÓGLAIGH NA hÉIREANN
FÓGRADH

An unprovoked attack with military forces has been made on the headquarters of our army in Dublin by forces under the control of a body describing themselves as the Provisional Government. It is possible that a similar attack may be made on us. We wish to make known to the citizens resident in our area that we have no desire to make war on any section of the Irish people.

Our policy from the beginning of the Volunteer movement (in 1913) has been to give protection to the people of Ireland against foreign aggression. We steadfastly followed this policy until the final declaration of Independence of Ireland and the establishment of the Irish Republic at the first meeting of An Dáil in January, 1919. As from that day we, at the bequest of the Irish people, acting through their freely elected representatives, have fought to maintain the Republic then established, and we have so far succeeded with the determined assistance, support and good-will of the Irish people – our sole aim and object now, as in the past, is to maintain the Republic intact.

We have no quarrel with Irish men and women. We wish to avoid any armed conflict with Irishmen.

Nevertheless, since a section of the Irish Army, calling themselves the forces of An Dáil, have attacked our forces (who have remained true to the ideals for which in the past men have fought and died), we deem it our duty to resist their attempt to subvert the Republic and to prevent them from achieving that which the British Imperial Army failed to achieve.

The Free State forces are being (as was openly stated in the British House of Commons) armed and equipped, and have been also offered assistance in men, by the British Government.

We, on the other hand, are regarded as the enemies of England and we must depend solely on ourselves and the people of Ireland. We are absolutely confident that, having Right and Principle on our side, and having as our comrades men who will rather die than surrender our unquestionable right to absolute independence, we shall win and that the People will stand by us in our fight for Freedom.

(Signed) T. Maguire
OC 2nd Western Division
Irish Republican Army

General Maguire's Proclamation, issued from Second Western Divisional Headquarters, Ballinrobe, Co Mayo on July 4 1922 and published in the Connaught Telegraph, *Castlebar on July 8. This followed the attack by Free State Forces on the General Headquarters, IRA, the Four Courts, Dublin on June 28. It declares his and his Division's allegiance to the All-Ireland Republic and their willingness to defend it from attack.*

dissolve itself and the Third Dáil could take over. Judge Diarmuid Crowley who ordered George Plunkett's release was later arrested. Judge Arthur Clery made the order on Eoin MacNeill absolute but the Republicans were powerless to put these orders into effect.

The Parliament of the All-Ireland Republic was suppressed. The Republican Courts were likewise subverted. The counter-revolution was well under way. It only remained to destroy the Army of the Republic – the Irish Republican Army. In 1996, 74 years later, that has not been accomplished and the All-Ireland Republic lives on through its last remaining organ, agency or structure.

Back in Co. Mayo, in that July of 1922, Tom Maguire and his men found themselves with no strong force opposing them. But the Free State Army advanced from Athlone. It now had artillery, armoured cars and immense firepower given over by the British. Personnel from the six disbanded British regiments in the 26 Counties had joined them, stiffening them as they faced their former comrades who had remained true to the Republic. Without pity or mercy they slew them. Generally former British officers were in charge of operations.

First Claremorris and then Castlebar were taken. The Free State forces landed by sea and took Westport. Tuam too was captured. Maguire says: "The rapid and businesslike way whereby the Free State gained control of the country, especially in areas where Republican garrisons were undecided on resistance was a major factor... It had a weakening effect on our effort."

"Here, as everywhere else, we adopted the strategy of evacuation. We had not the material, so we retired from the barracks and made for the hills." Ballinrobe barracks was burned first to prevent its being used by the Free State. The moral to the material may be as three is to one, as Napoleon is credited with saying. But in the Free State War in Ireland, as in the Spanish War 1936-39, the sheer weight of metal told.

Maguire says there was no cohesion or military council formed between the military commanders in the West, Liam Pilkington of the Third, Michael Kilroy of the Fourth and himself. When a Western Command was established in 1923 to co-ordinate action, it was too late.

The Republican strategy was wholly defensive which has been described as the death of any revolution. A few attacks were made on the Free State in the Second Western area but nothing spectacular was undertaken. The thinking or the willpower that had created the ambushes of a year-and-a-half earlier were no longer there.

"You could not bring yourself to want this sort of warfare," says Tom Maguire, "The British were the enemy, the old enemy; there was a certain pride in having the ability to attack them. That feeling was entirely absent in the Civil War. We knew the Free State Army comprising 50,000 newly recruited mercenaries would not hesitate to shoot us, but that made it no easier for us to pluck up enough anger to really fight them. And the people themselves were disheartened."

On a personal note, he said: "When I heard of the deaths of people on the Free State side like Griffith, Collins, Seán Hales, I could not be glad. You felt these are people who fought the British and now they are gone. Britain is really the victor."

Finally, more than 10 weeks after the Second Dáil was to meet and dissolve and the Third Dáil to assemble, a parliament did convene in Dublin – this time at Leinster House. It turned out to be "the House of Parliament to which the Provisional Government is to be responsible" and not the Second or the Third All-Ireland Dáil.

Republicans wished Seán O'Mahony to go and claim his seat as representative of Fermanagh-Tyrone, because his exclusion would expose the 26-County Assembly for what it was and as a breach of the Collins-de Valera Pact. He decided not to go. But another Republican went there, the 68-year-old Larry Ginnell, veteran land agitator and Deputy for Longford-Westmeath.

As an independent nationalist MP he had been many times ejected from the British House of Commons for asking questions to which it did not suit Ministers to reply. For September 9 he gave notice of several important motions, including a categorical vote of censure upon those Deputies who "having no authority to change policy, least of all from peace to war... did illegally usurp authority as a government and establish themselves as military dictators... did illegally at the bidding of a foreign government begin civil war... did illegally by decree purport to suppress the Supreme Court of the Republic... and are steadily overthrowing Dáil Éireann and substituting their own personal government."[7]

If it were Dáil Éireann was in session, he would sign the roll and take his seat. But the Oath of Allegiance to the Republic was not being administered and there was no reply when he asked: "Is this Dáil Éireann or a Partition Parliament? Is this Dáil for the whole of Ireland? If the Republican member for Fermanagh attends here will he be heard?"[8] He persisted and was forcibly dragged out. His question had been answered, though not by words.

The English King's representative in Ireland, the Lord Lieutenant, Viscount FitzAlan sent a letter to Leinster House saying the Parliament had his best wishes and prayers. The Labour Party acted as an opposition while the newly shuffled Provisional Government put through a British-dictated constitution for the "Irish Free State".

At the same time they passed the "Army Powers Resolution" called the Murder Act setting up secret military courts with power of life and death. Mulcahy argued it was necessary to give the troops power to kill their prisoners in an authorised way in order "to prevent men from taking on themselves authority to execute people in an unauthorised way".

Republican Deputies had been killed, Harry Boland during his arrest while unarmed and Séamus Devins, TD for Sligo-Mayo East after capture on active service on Ben Bulben mountain. With Brigadier Devins TD were murdered five other Volunteers including Brian Mac Neill, Divisional Adjutant and son of Eoin Mac Neill now a Free State Minister.

Others were murdered while prisoners, notably in Dublin, before the military courts sitting in secret began to function on October 15.

Some days after this Tom Maguire was captured in a dug-out in the Headford area of North Galway. With him was Divisional Engineer Michael Martyn. "It was then," says Tom, "that I really experienced the sort of mercenaries they were, ex-British Army soldiers, tramps and misfits of every conceivable type." The Free State Army was now over 50,000 strong.

Tom was taken to the former British military barracks in Athlone where there were two prison-camps; one known as Pump Square for ordinary detainees and another, Garrison Detention for those captured after the Murder Act was passed. Tom Maguire was held in the latter camp, which had regular cells, having been captured in arms.

Meanwhile, the Catholic Hierarchy in a "Joint-Pastoral" Letter condemned resistance to the Provisional Government and stigmatised the war by the Republican side as "a system of murder and assassination". The oath to the Republic was not binding, it said, and spoke of "unauthorised murder". When is murder authorised, asked Republicans and the ill-chosen words were repudiated by their own authors.

The sacraments were refused to Republicans and church doors were shut against their dead bodies. Over 10,000 prisoners were banned from the sacraments by the bare fact that they were in prison – half without charge of any kind. Priests who came out into the open as Republicans like Capuchins Father Albert and Father Dominic were driven into exile. Fr Pádraig de Brún, Professor of Mathematics at Maynooth, was imprisoned. Fr Michael O'Flanagan when he returned from a speaking tour of Australia and the US was silenced. Others did good by stealth.

By October 25 the new Free State constitution was voted through the Provisional Parliament for 26 Counties. However, on that day also the Government of the All-Ireland Republic was re-constituted. The available Republican Deputies met secretly in Dublin, constituted themselves as the Republican Government and appointed De Valera President. A Council of State of twelve members was also appointed.

An Army Proclamation of October 28 proclaimed De Valera to be President of the Republic and named the twelve Deputies making up the Council of State. The Cabinet these would appoint would be temporarily the Supreme Executive until the Parliament of the Republic could freely assemble. The Army pledged its allegiance and support to this authority.

This was done by the Army Executive, the Proclamation stated "In the spirit of our oath as the final custodians of the Republic..." Thirteen senior officers, members of the IRA Executive, signed the Proclamation. The view taken by the Deputies who assembled was that those who remained faithful to the Republic and to the Republican oath now constituted the Second Dáil.

An Emergency Government was formed and Ministers of State appointed. The action taken by the Republican Army and Deputies was in accordance with a resolution of the First Dáil of March 11, 1921 which provided that if

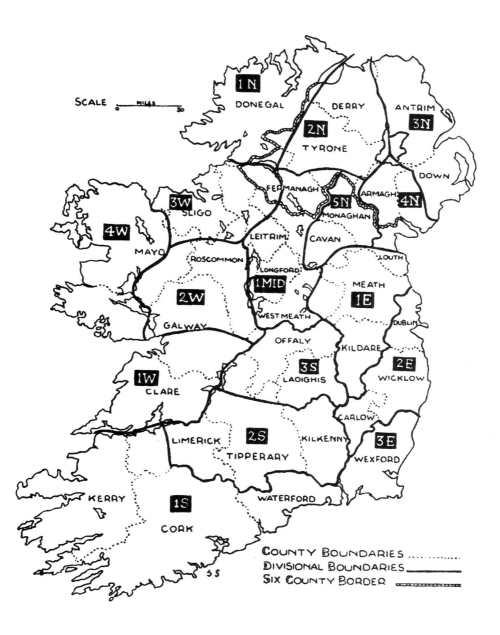

SCALE

COUNTY BOUNDARIES ....
DIVISIONAL BOUNDARIES _____
SIX COUNTY BORDER ≈≈≈≈≈≈≈≈

IRA Divisional Areas 1921-23,
reprinted from No Other Law.

enemy action ever succeeded in preventing the Dáil from functioning democratically, the Army should have power to proclaim an emergency government,

The Republic, after a lapse of several months, was no longer without a government. However, although it had the support of a large portion of the population as the only *de jure* (rightful or lawful) government it was unable to function as such. It did represent the protest against the *coup d'état* or seizure of power by the Free State party and it maintained the continuity of the All-Ireland Republic.

It also placed the logical and constitutional facts of the situation on the record by means of statements and proclamations issued from time to time. Liam Mellows in his *Notes from Mountjoy Jail* at the end of August had advocated the establishment of such a government as the necessary and logical step, providing among other things a rallying point for all Republicans and pro-national independence forces.

The Free State response was to commence executing Republican prisoners. Relatives were not informed officially and had not even been aware of a "trial" by military court. The press report of execution was often the first intimation they had. A letter of protest and warning was addressed to the "Speaker of the Provisional Parliament of Southern Ireland" on November 27 signed by Liam Lynch, Chief-of-Staff, on behalf of the Army Council, Óglaigh na hÉireann.

It protested against the abandonment of the recognised rules of warfare by the Free State Army and the barbarous treatment of prisoners by them. The members of the Provisional Government and the members of its parliament who voted for the resolution "pretending to make legal the murder of soldiers" were all guilty and unless such action stopped "very drastic measures" would be adopted. Further executions, retaliation as promised and execution of Republican leaders without any semblance of a trial followed.

In Tom Maguire's case, he was courtmartialled in January 1923. "The court," he says, "was a military one although they were all in civvies. I enquired when I was brought in 'What is this?' although I knew damned well. 'I do not recognise this court,' I answered, 'you have no authority to try me.' They went through their rigmarole of accusations nonetheless, and of course they found me guilty."

On January 19, Tom and five others of his command were put into special cells before lock-up. Next morning the five were taken out and shot by firing squad. Tom Maguire was not. He could not tell why. "Unless it was because I was popular. I did have a reputation for fair play. During the Tan struggle unionists and loyalists could call upon me if someone was trying to lean upon them."

"I was a TD," he continues, "but that had not saved Mellows or Childers, and I did not expect it would save me." (Liam Mellows and Erskine Childers were not in fact returned to the Third Dáil in June 1922). But the Free State did something else. They captured 18 Volunteers in North Galway in February. Following an IRA attack on a Free State post at Headford in April, six of these were picked out and executed at Tuam. Tom Maguire's younger brother Seán was one of the six.

With the Chief-of-Staff, Liam Lynch, killed in action that April and the military situation an impossible one, the Army Executive met. Later the Army Council and the Republican Government had a joint meeting and decided to terminate armed resistance to Free State forces. On the 27th a Proclamation from the Second Dáil and a Special Army Order suspended the offensive from April 30, 1923.

Nevertheless, executions continued, Republican soldiers were hunted down and killed, notably Niall "Plunkett" O'Boyle during a parley with Free State troops at Knocknadruce, Co Wicklow. The peace efforts being attempted came to nothing. These were on the basis that:

1. "The sovereignty of the Irish Nation and the integrity of its territory are inalienable and

2. "That any instrument purporting to the contrary is, to the extent of its violation of the above principle, null and void."

These were the terms of the Army Executive for peace with the Free State. They were rejected. On May 24, a Cease Fire Order was issued by the new Chief-of-Staff, Frank Aiken, to all ranks. Arms were to be dumped. These decisions were the outcome of another meeting of the Republican Cabinet and the Army Council; the war would not be renewed but arms would not be surrendered. They were to be stored in concealment as safely as possible from discovery.

On June 10, Tom Maguire and five comrades escaped from Athlone military barracks. They made their way northwards into Co Roscommon and found that the confusion among the people had been cleared away by the executions. But of course, it was too late at that stage. Tom was back in his old divisional area and was re-appointed GOC Second Western Division, IRA.

He was also re-appointed to the Army Executive and attended its meeting on July 11-12 when re-organisation plans were set in motion and preparations made for the impending General Election in the 26 Counties. Before that took place on August 25, one of the six who had escaped with Tom, Toby Mannion of The Berries, Athlone was shot by Free State officers while unarmed.

"Shoot-on-sight" was still in operation and 12,000 prisoners were in jails and prison camps as the election was under way. De Valera was shot at and then arrested in Ennis while the Sinn Féin Director of Elections, Éamon Donnelly, was arrested in Dublin and jailed. Tom Maguire stood for the new constituency of Mayo South and was elected.

He recounts: "I was being opposed on this my third appearance before the electorate, but I won nevertheless. Sinn Féin did much better, coming back with 44 seats. There was no fairness in the election. I could make no public appearances although I chanced one or two.

"George Maguire of Claremorris, my election agent, told me afterwards that bundles of votes intended for me were put to one side as spoiled. When he asked to inspect these he was assaulted. Two-and-a-half miles from here (Cross, Co Mayo) in Glencorrib, the presiding officer, a local teacher, was obliged to leave the polling station because of rowdiness from Free State supporters."

THE SECOND
FREE STATE PARTY

ALL THIS TIME, Tom Maguire was on the run and remained so until December 1924 when he married Christina Feeney of Ballinrobe, sister of Pádraic Feeney, murdered by British Forces at Tourmakeady while a prisoner on the day of the famous ambush.

De Valera, he related, visited Rome with his secretary Seán MacBride the following year. He met there Archbishop Mannix of Melbourne, Australia and Monsignor O'Hagan, Rector of the Irish College in Rome. They convinced him to recognise the existing political institutions and enter Leinster House. He never reported on this meeting to the Ard-Chomhairle of Sinn Féin or to the Second Dáil, which still met regularly.

Maguire goes on: "In any case, fearing what was about to happen following the resignation of its Chief-of-Staff, the IRA reverted to its independent status, free of any control by Sinn Féin. Thus it returned to the position it had held prior to August 1919 and for nine months during 1922." The Army Convention of November 1925 forced Aiken to resign. It also broke with the Second Dáil as the Republican Government because it feared a repetition of the betrayal of 1922.

Tom Maguire speaks of his personal situation at the time of his marriage. There was an economic boycott of Republicans which led to an exodus by them on the emigrant ships. "We were just building this house again and it was not quite finished. It was a hard, hungry time.

"My father's business was wrecked. They had stolen or taken away the models or templates for wheels that are so necessary in this trade. So it was hard for me to start back again." Tom was in his 34th year, his father nearly 70. They did not start up the coach-building again. Tom Maguire became an insurance broker.

"After 1925," he says, "you had the virtual dissolution of this thriving political party with 44 seats in the South to create Fianna Fáil." In fact Sinn Féin had won four more seats at by-elections since 1923, bringing their total to 48. In *The Irish Republic*, p 803 Dorothy Macardle says: "In every one of twelve by-elections since August 1923, the

"The Turning of the Tide"

Referring to five by-elections in November, 1924, Dorothy Macardle says: "In each of the constituencies the Republican vote showed an increase; there was a total Republican gain, as compared with the General Election of 1923, of over 29,000 votes" (p802).

In March, 1925 more by-elections took place. Dorothy Macardle sums up:

"In every one of the twelve by-elections held since August 1923, the Republican vote had shown an increase over the General Election result. For this there were more reasons than one; there was less interference with Sinn Féin's organisation, many supporters of the Treaty disliked the repressive measures which the (Free State) Government employed; but the outstanding factor was, undoubtedly, that the people were recovering their courage and equipoise.

"Whatever the causes, the truth was manifest: the tide had already turned in Ireland; the ebb that had begun with the signing of the Treaty was already over and the Flow, however slow and gradual, had begun." (pp 803-4)

– *The Irish Republic*

Republican vote had shown an increase over the General Election vote." In many cases this was substantial and Sinn Féin also retained two seats North of the Border in 1925.

The break in 1926 was almost inevitable, Tom says, once De Valera had made his decision to take part in Leinster House and the Belfast parliament. Accepting the two partition states was to be "a question of policy not of principle" once the oath to the British Crown was removed.

He continues: "My main objection to Leinster House was that it was a British institution and a lowering of the flag. I said this at a meeting of the Second Dáil early, as far as I can recall now, in 1926. De Valera who was present resented this. 'It is not a lowering of the flag,' he interjected. It reminded him painfully, I knew, of his own statement in October 1917 when he had been elected President of Sinn Féin in succession to Arthur Griffith: 'We say it is necessary to be united under the flag under which we are going to fight for freedom – the flag of the Irish Republic. We have nailed that flag to the mast, we shall never lower it.'

"Our hope after 1923, and the organisation's policy, was simply to go on increasing our strength which we had been doing. When we had reached a majority, in other words after another 20 seats or so, we could reconvene the Third Dáil and proceed away from the Treaty position. That was agreed by De Valera and everybody else within the organi-

Photo taken at Easter 1928 following a meeting of the Second (All-Ireland) Dáil Éireann elected in 1921 and never dissolved. Even after the defection of Fianna Fáil the previous year there was still a quorum present to transmit business. This photo hung in Tom Maguire's livingroom and was proudly shown to visitors.

Members present were: (front row) Phil Shanahan (Dublin Mid); Prof W. F. P. Stockley (National University of Ireland); Mrs Kate O'Callaghan (Limerick City and Limerick East); Art O'Connor (Kildare and Wicklow); J. J. O'Kelly (Louth and Meath); Mary Mac Swiney (Cork City); Dáithí Ceannt (Cork North-East and East); George Count Plunkett (Leitrim and Roscommon North); Brian O'Higgins (Clare);

(second row) Count O'Byrne (Tipperary South, North and Mid); Éamonn Dee (Waterford); Séamus Lennon (Carlow and Kilkenny); M. P. Colivet (Limerick City and Limerick East); Austin Stack (Kerry and West Limerick); Charles Murphy (Dublin South); Seán O'Mahony (Fermanagh and Tyrone); Dr Ada English (National University of Ireland); Thomas O'Donoghue (Kerry and West Limerick); Dr J. Crowley (Mayo North and West);

(back row) Thomas Maguire (Mayo South and Roscommon South); Seán Mac Swiney (Co Cork West, South and Mid); Seán O'Farrell (Sligo and Leitrim); Brian Mellows (Galway); Mrs Caitlín Brugha (Waterford); Mrs Eileen Tubberd, stenographer and Dublin City Councillor Joe Clarke, courier. Seán O'Farrell, Brian Mellows and Mrs Brugha, having been elected in 1923, were not members of the Second Dáil.

sation. He breached that policy although he could have reverted to it – and gained the wholehearted support of Republican Ireland – if he had taken it up again in 1932."

In the event, De Valera failed to get a majority at the Extraordinary Ard-Fheis of Sinn Féin in March 1926 and resigned as President next day. In May he formed Fianna Fáil – and confined its organisation to the 26 Counties. He failed also to get a majority of the Deputies of the Second Dáil and resigned as President of the Republic.

He continued with his supporters to attend meetings of the Second Dáil – presumably so that he could acquire the US funds subscribed to the First and Second Dáil Loans[9] – until the summer of 1927 after which he entered Leinster House, swallowing the oath in the process.

Tom Maguire was by then no longer on the Executive of the IRA. "They seemed to be giving Fianna Fáil a certain measure of support," he says. In the June, 1927 General Election in the 26 Counties, the IRA officially withdrew support from both Sinn Féin and Fianna Fáil. They forbade Tom to stand for Sinn Féin again, even though he wished to do so. South Mayo was therefore not even contested by Sinn Féin. However, in the other constituency in the county, North Mayo, Dr John A Madden – a veteran soldier of both the Black-and-Tan and Free State Wars – was returned for Sinn Féin. Squeezed between the IRA and Fianna Fáil, Sinn Féin did badly. It held five seats only[10], plus two independent Republican abstentionists, to Fianna Fáil's 44.

Then in July the Electoral Amendment Bill was put through Leinster House. It required candidates in future elections to swear they would take the oath. That drove Sinn Féin and people like Tom Maguire out of public life and opened the way further for Fianna Fáil.

The *Irish Times* of July 26, 1927 quotes De Valera as saying: "Under no circumstances whatever would I subscribe to such an oath; that is final." Sixteen days later on August 11, he and his party did so.

Meanwhile, the Second Dáil had elected Art O'Connor as President of the Republic. When he resigned in December 1927, the office was allowed to lapse and an Executive Council of Dáil Éireann was elected instead. Personalities had cost them dearly. The six members of that Executive were: Count Plunkett, Mary Mac Swiney, Dáithí Ceannt, Brian O'Higgins, Cathal Ó Murchadha, plus Seán Ó Ceallaigh (Sceilg), Ceann Comhairle ex officio.[11]

With the departure of Michael Kilroy of West Mayo to Fianna Fáil Tom Maguire took over organisation and training of the Irish Republican Army in that area as well as in his own South Mayo. He also continued as a member of the Second Dáil.

They remained on after 1926 in Tom's words "as a shadow government in the same shadowy form in which we had existed since 1922", making statements on the great questions of the day to the Irish people and continuing the Republican position. A photograph taken after their Easter 1928 meeting showed that with 21 Deputies of the Dáil elected in 1921 still meeting in allegiance to the All-Ireland Republic they still had the necessary quorum to transact business.

That photo hung in the living-room of Tom Maguire's home in Cross until his death.[12] At that session on April 29, 1928 membership of the Executive Council was increased to eight, An Ceann Comhairle as an ex officio member acting as Cathaoirleach.[13]

ALL-IRELAND DÁIL
FUNCTIONS UNTIL 1938

AT THE TENTH anniversary of the First (All-Ireland) Dáil, on January 22, 1929 Mary Mac Swiney introduced a Bill for the Constitution of the Republic of Ireland to a meeting of the Second Dáil. According to J. Bowyer Bell in *The Secret Army* this was "the major governmental project during 1929" and "much of the year was given to discussion and publication of the details of the ideal Republican government". Mary Mac Swiney's constitution, as it is called, was adopted by the Second Dáil; it makes interesting reading even today.

On March 14 that year, De Valera made a remarkable statement in the Free State Parliament. "I still hold that our right to be regarded as the legitimate Government of this country is faulty, that this House itself is faulty. You have secured a *de facto* position". He accused the Free State of having brought off a *coup d'état* in the summer of 1922 and stated: "Those who have continued on in that organisation which we have left can claim exactly the same continuity that we claimed up to 1925. They can do it..." (Those interested can read the full text of De Valera's remarks in T. P. Coogan's *The IRA* pp 56 and 57 or the Second Dáil's statement of April 16, 1932).

Tom Maguire did not have anything to do with Saor Éire, the short-lived political organisation which the IRA in 1931 sought to have as the political wing of the Republican Movement instead of Sinn Féin. When Seán Ó Ceallaigh (Sceilg) stepped down as President of Sinn Féin at the Ard Fheis on October 4 of that year and Brian O'Higgins (Brian na Banban) replaced him, Tom Maguire became Vice-President.

In 1932 he was chosen to give the oration at the annual Wolfe Tone Commemoration in Bodenstown, County Kildare and resisted an attempt by Mick Price, an IRA leader, to give him directions as to what he should say. "My answer was that whenever in the past I had spoken in public, I did not require to seek inspiration from others. Mick was not going to write my speech for me and I told him that." Maguire was direct and to the point as usual.

Earlier that year of 1932 a "special session of Dáil Éire-

DÁIL ÉIREANN

GOVERNMENT OF THE REPUBLIC OF IRELAND.

16, Sráid Pairneill,
Baile Áta Cliat.

16, Parnell Sq.,
Dublin.

A special session of Dáil Éireann held on Saturday, April 2, 1932, was attended by Seán Ó Ceallaigh (Ceann Comhairle), Miss Mary McSwiney, Count Plnnkett, Sean O'Mahony, Brian O'Huiginn, Tom McGuire and Cathal O'Murchadha of the Executive Council; Mrs. O'Callaghan, Count O'Byrne, Professor Stockley, and Tomás O'Donoghue. Deputies Mrs. Cathal Brugha, Dr. Kathleen Lynn, Dr. Madden, Sean O'Farrell and Sean Buckley were also present.

Letters regretting inability to attend were read from Dr. Crowley, Sean MacSwiney, and Seamus Lennon.

A vote of sympathy with the relatives of the late Deputy Tom Hunter was passed in silence.

Important proposals from the Republican Organizations of Northern Ireland were before the Assembly and appropriate action indicated.

Dr. Madden drew attention to the very irregular distribution of land in the West, and it transpired from the discussion that the evil was widespread.

Consideration was given to the question of the seizure from a Dublin Bank by the British Government of Republican funds to the extent of £20,000, and of the Sinn Fein funds amounting to some £10,000 still retained in Chancery.

It was decided, after a very full discussion, to issue the following statement on the existing situation:

Front cover of the Official Report of the meeting of the Second (All-Ireland) Dáil, held on April 2, 1932.

ann" (the revolutionary Second Dáil) was held on April 2. According to the official report published in Dublin on April 16 it "was attended by Seán Ó Ceallaigh (Ceann Comhairle), Miss Mary Mac Swiney, Count Plunkett, Seán O'Mahony, Brian Ó hUiginn, Tom McGuire (sic) and Cathal Ó Murchadha of the Executive Council; Mrs O'Callaghan, Count O'Byrne, Professor Stockley, and Tomás O'Donoghue. Deputies Mrs Cathal Brugha, Dr Kathleen Lynn, Dr Madden, Seán O'Farrell and Seán Buckley were also present. Letters regretting inability to attend were read from Dr Crowley, Seán Mac Swiney and Séamus Lennon. A note of sympathy with the relatives of the late Deputy Thomas Hunter was passed in silence."

All but five of those mentioned above had been elected in 1921 to the Second (All-Ireland) Dáil which was suppressed by the Free State but was never dissolved and remained on as the shadow government of the Republic. The five, Caitlín Brugha, Dr Lynn, Dr Madden, Seán O'Farrell and Seán Buckley[14] were elected as Sinn Féin Deputies in 1923 or 1927. They were abstentionists from the Free State Parliament, of course, since they denied its legitimacy but stood ready to take their seats in the Third (All-Ireland) Dáil when such would be assembled.

The position of the two Sinn Féin candidates elected North of the Border in 1925 was similar as was that of Pádraig Mac Lógáin, later President of Sinn Féin in 1950-53 and '54-'62, when he was elected for South Armagh as a Republican candidate in 1933. Following the latter success Stormont introduced a new measure precluding the nomination of Republicans in elections held by it or in local elections.

Incidentally, the position of the six Sinn Féin TDs[15] elected North and South of the Border in 1955 and 1957 was exactly the same. The two elected for Mid-Ulster and Fermanagh-South Tyrone were always described as TDs, members of the All-Ireland Parliament to come, or simply Republican Deputies. They were never described in the Movement as "MPs" as they did not regard themselves as members of the British Parliament.

Similarly, despite descriptions to the contrary, true Republicans never called those elected in 1981, '82 or '83 Stormont Assembly members, MPs or members of Leinster House. All were members of the Republican Movement, whether elected as H-Block or Sinn Féin candidates, and all were in fact Republican Deputies to an All-Ireland Parliament, the Third Dáil Éireann. Whether elected in the '30s, '50s or '80s these were constituent, component parts of the new 32-County Government - yet to be achieved.

The report of the April 1932 meeting of the Second Dáil went on to say, somewhat cryptically, that "important proposals from the Republican Organisations of Northern Ireland (sic) were before the Assembly and appropriate action indicated." Defence discussions, proposals or decisions were never recorded in the minutes of the First or Second Dáil from 1919 onwards, it is of interest to note.

Other questions were raised too: "Dr Madden drew attention to the very irregular distribution of land in the West, and it transpired from the discussion that the evil was widespread." Finance was of course on the agenda: "Consideration was given to the question of the seizure from a Dublin bank by the British Government of Republican funds to the extent of £20,000, and of the Sinn Féin funds amounting to some £10,000 still retained in (Free State) Chancery."

Following "a very full discussion", a comprehensive statement was issued on the "existing situation. It referred to England's record on so-called Treaties, the Land Annuities (then a very live issue), England's Debt to Ireland, Free State Exploitation of Aonach Tailteann and De Valera's Definition of the Status of Dáil Éireann in 1924 and 1929. In the autumn of 1924 the recently released President (De Valera) was quoted as stating to the Second Dáil that they would "be ready to take over control when the people turned down the existing junta."

De Valera went on to say that " the position of the Deputy for Fermanagh was the symbol of the unity of the country. The Second Dáil," he added, "was not yet dissolved, nor was the Third Dáil legally summoned." Having quoted very fully de Valera's remarks in the Free State parliament in March 1929, already referred to, the statement ended with a clarion call "warning the nation's youth against the futility of compromise". It concluded: "Let the aim of all self-reliant citizens be One Army and One Government for all Ireland – the Army and the Government of the Irish Republic."

In his interview in *Survivors*, Tom Maguire says: "I had nothing to do with the Bass Boycott of 1932, nor with the Republican Congress in 1934. I put no faith in Fianna Fáil, although I hoped they would improve the country economically. They did a lot of political window-dressing, but it never impressed me." Tom was otherwise active. One West Of Ireland Republican[16] who was present at the annual Co Mayo Easter Commemoration in Castlebar in 1935 remembers Tom speaking there. "Very impressive, with military bearing, tall, dignified and straight as an arrow" was his description of the hero of the Tourmakeady Ambush.

When the Republican Movement contested two by-elections in 1936, in Co. Galway and Co. Wexford, Tom Maguire worked for the veteran Count Plunkett who was the candidate in Co. Galway. The IRA had launched another short-lived political wing, Cumann Poblachta na hÉireann and both it and Sinn Féin campaigned for Count Plunkett. The Oath of Allegiance to the King of England had been removed by De Valera in 1933 and Republicans were free to nominate once more in the 26 Counties. However hard Mary Mac Swiney, Tom Maguire, Count Plunkett and their followers worked, the fact remained that the Republicans had been excluded from parliamentary elections for a decade and electoral support had dwindled. Fianna Fáil and Fine Gael swamped them.

Time had taken its toll too of the faithful Deputies of the Second Dáil. Austin Stack, former Kerry All-Ireland footballer and Minister for Home Affairs in the First and Second Dáil had died aged 49 in 1929. He had remained at his post as General Secretary of Sinn Féin from 1917 until his early death – his health undermined by jail protests and no less than five hunger-strikes for political treatment. In 1930 the veteran survivor of the gallant Kent family of Fermoy, Co. Cork, Dáithí Ceannt – crippled since 1916 by British bullets – passed on. Seán O'Mahony, Republican Deputy for Fermanagh who was excluded from the Free State Parliament, died in 1934.

The latter two had been members of the Executive Council of the All-Ireland Dáil, Dáithí Ceannt from its inception in December 1927 and Seán O'Mahony sometime between April 1928 and 1932. Tom Maguire had become an Executive Council member before 1932 and Professor William Stockley of UCC was elected to it between 1932 and 1938 when it met for the last time.

POWERS OF GOVERNMENT
DELEGATED TO IRA

IN DECEMBER OF 1938 the IRA was about to launch its military campaign in England. The leadership, the Army Council, approached the Executive Council of the Second Dáil with a view to having the Dáil's executive powers delegated to the Army "to be held in trust" by it. This most important event took place on December 8, 1938 and was the subject of a special proclamation carried by the Wolfe Tone Weekly in its issue of December 17.[17]

The First (All-Ireland) Dáil meeting on March 11, 1921 at the height of the Black-and-Tan War had resolved that when enemy action had reduced the House to five Deputies, that "it should resolve itself into a Provisional Government" and that "Government should be left to the Volunteers as the Military Body" which was usual in the case of countries invaded.

In October 1922, the faithful Deputies of the last 32-County Dáil constituted an "Emergency Government" with the support of the IRA. Those who had betrayed the Republic and made war on it were regarded as having forfeited membership of the All-Ireland Dáil.

The final meeting, in 1938, of the Executive Council of the 1921 Dáil was presided over by Sceilg (Seán Ó Ceallaigh), Ceann Comhairle. It resolved "We hereby delegate the authority reposed in us to the Army Council in the spirit of the decision taken by Dáil Éireann in the Spring of 1921."

Their proclamation went on "Confident, in delegating this sacred trust to the Army of the Republic, that in their every action towards its consummation they will be inspired by the high ideals and the chivalry of our martyred comrades, we, as the Executive Council of Dáil Éireann, Government of the Republic, append our names."

The reply of the Army Council following its meeting on December 8 of that year was signed by the Chairman and Secretary. It stated: "We accept this authority in the name of the Army of the Republic in the spirit in which it is tendered." Brian P Murphy comments: "The signing of this document brings to a close a chapter in the struggle for the title of republican authenticity."[18]

QUESTION OF SUBSTITUTES FOR MEMBERS ARRESTED.

The PRESIDENT said their next business was to make provision for carrying on their work. Their numbers would not be increasing for some time and a situation might arise if their numbers went very low. He would like to hear their views on the appointing of Substitutes. Of course it would be irregular and wholly unconstitutional, but they would have a body to speak for the country.

The ASSISTANT MINISTER FOR DEFENCE suggested that each member would nominate a substitute to be ratified by the local Comhairle Ceanntair.

P. O'KEEFFE (Cork, North) pointed out most of the best men in the Comhairli Ceanntair were on the run or in jail.

After considerable discussion COUNT PLUNKETT (Roscommon, North) said that the Government should be left to the Military Body when the membership of the Dáil was reduced to a certain figure. It was usual to substitute military dictatorship in countries invaded; and instead of the House appointing substitutes, it should be left to the Volunteers as the Military Body. They should be authorised by this House to establish a Provisional Government.

J. BURKE (Tipperary, Mid.) agreed with the suggestion and said if the Dáil was going to carry on it was essential that it should maintain its representative character. If substitutes were appointed it would affect the authority of the Dáil in the eyes of the public.

J. MACENTEE (Monaghan, South) suggested they should fix the number at which the Dáil should resolve itself into a Provisional Government.

The PRESIDENT suggested that when the number fell to five the Army should take control.

The ACTING SPEAKER took the sense of the House on the proposal that the Dáil continue to function until its membership was reduced to five, and that it should then resolve itself into a Provisional Government.

The House accepted the proposition without dissent, and it was intimated that the matter could be further discussed at next Session.

Extract from the Minutes of the meeting of the First (All-Ireland) Dáil, March 11, 1921. It was on the basis of this resolution that the powers of government were delegated to the Army Council of the IRA in 1938.

The surviving faithful Deputies who constituted the Executive Council of the Second (All-Ireland) Dáil were named as: Seán Ó Ceallaigh, "Sceilg", (Louth-Meath); Count Plunkett (Leitrim-North Roscommon); Cathal Ó Murchadha (Dublin South); Tom Maguire (South Mayo-South Roscommon); Mary Mac Swiney (Cork City); Brian Ó hUiginn (Clare) and Prof W. F. P. Stockley (National University of Ireland).

Tom Maguire was opposed to this move at first. When it was put to him "is this not the recognition of the Republic that we all seek", he signified agreement and the decision was unanimous on both sides. Tom's loyalty to the All-Ireland Republic was to be tested severely twice more before his long life came to an end. He would stand alone and defiant, faithful to the end.

In April, 1940 he attended the funeral of Comdt Tony Darcy to the Republican Plot in Donaghpatrick Cemetery, Headford, Co. Galway. Darcy (32) had been OC Galway Battalion IRA and was later OC Western Command. He died on hunger strike for political treatment while a prisoner in St Bricin's Military Hospital, Arbour Hill, Dublin.

Tom was present when Darcy was buried beside Seán Maguire and the other Republicans executed in Tuam and Athlone in 1923. Free State troops in combat gear with fixed bayonets ringed the cemetery supported by armoured cars and machine gun crews while police held the gates and refused admittance except to the coffin and Darcy's widow and three young children.

The huge turnout climbed the comparatively low cemetery walls and hand-to-hand fighting took place on a wide scale as Free State forces attacked the mourners. Tom often recounted these disgraceful scenes when the burial was interrupted and even the gravediggers set upon. Máirtín Ó Cadhain, the famous Irish writer, presided at the graveside during the mêlée and Maurice Twomey, IRA Chief-of-Staff 1927-36, gave the oration. Máirtín was arrested in Headford that evening and interned without trial. The grave in the Republican Plot was not filled in properly until the following day.

This was the post at Donaghpatrick where Tom Maguire now acted as the local keeper of the flame. With the mass internments and jailings of Republicans on both sides of the Border and more than 100 imprisoned in England arising out of the 1939-40 IRA Bombing Campaign there,

The members of the Executive Council of Dáil Éireann (32 Counties) who delegated the Government of the Irish Republic to the Army Council of the Irish Republican Army, on December 8, 1938: (left to right from the top) Seán Ó Ceallaigh, Ceann Comhairle; George Count Plunkett; Professor William Stockley; Mary Mac Swiney; Brian Ó hUiginn; Tom Maguire; Cathal Ó Murchadha.

there was danger that the annual Easter Commemorations in each county would lapse.

Older veterans who were at liberty came forward and kept the continuity. In North Galway Tom Maguire held the torch once more. Now in his fifties, he cycled each Easter from his home in Cross, a distance of more than ten miles, to the Plot in Donaghpatrick to speak the oration during all the oppressive and lean times from 1941 to 1954. In 1955 a new generation of Galway people took over these Republican duties.

At Easter that year Tom was at Drumboe, Stranorlar, Co. Donegal where he unveiled a memorial cross at the spot where four Republican soldiers had been buried in 1923 after execution by Free State forces. The most prominent of these, Comdt-Gen Charlie Daly of Firies, Co. Kerry had been GOC Second Northern Division, IRA during the Black-and-Tan War and GOC First Northern Division in the War against the Free State. He was a good friend of Tom Maguire in those years. The others also executed by firing squad there were Brigadier Seán Larkin "from the banks of the Roe" at the Loup, Magherafelt, Co. Derry and Lieuts Tim O'Sullivan and Dan Enright from Listowel, Co. Kerry.

Earlier, in August 1952 Tom had unveiled an imposing memorial at the Republican Plot in Donaghpatrick Cemetery. It was erected by a committee of North Galway Republicans and designed by two old comrades of Tom's, John Henaghan of Tuam and Mick Martyn of Galway city. The latter had been Divisional Engineer under Maguire and was captured with him in a dug-out in October 1922, it will be remembered.

Speaking to an assembly of 5,000 people at the graveside of eleven of his command done to death by the 26-County state, Comdt-Gen Maguire said:[19] "I appeal to the youth especially to follow in the footsteps of those brave men and not to be led astray by the false promises of politicians and collaborators.

"It is no shame to the men buried here or in the hundreds of such graves all over Ireland that the attainment of an Irish Republic is still unfinished and that Six Counties remain occupied by the enemy. Those shackles must be broken if we are to be true to the memory of all those generations who have died for Ireland."

From then on Tom Maguire was guest speaker at the

ESCALATOR UP TO
IN⋅⋅RNATIONAL DEPARTURE LOBBY   DOMESTIC TERMINALS
FC⋅⋅GN EXCHANGE SERVICE   AIR ⋅   RESTAURANTS   ↑

Accompanied by Eoin McNamee, Tyrone, General Chairman of the Fenian Centenary Committee, General Tom Maguire is received by Clan na Gael Guards on his arrival at O'Hare Airport, Chicago, to deliver the oration on Easter Sunday, 1967.

unveiling of many memorials to the Republican dead and at the funerals of his deceased comrades. In September, 1963 he officiated at the unveiling of the massive Co. Roscommon IRA Memorial at Shankill Cross, Elphin, honouring 40 Volunteers who died for the All-Ireland Republic.

The South Roscommon Brigade had been in Tom's Second Western Division and the North Roscommon Brigade in the Third Western under Liam Pilkington of Sligo. Pilkington had long been a Catholic priest and, ever faithful to the Republican Cause, he sent a message from his parish in Monmouthshire, Wales to be read out on the great occasion.

The chairman that day, Seosamh Ó Ceallaigh of Ballaghaderreen, an active Republican since 1916, died three years later and Tom, his old comrade, spoke at his graveside. In 1968 he unveiled a monument in Kilconnell Abbey, East Galway to Michael Silke, a local man who had been Chief of Republican Police in Co. Sligo in 1920-21 and was interned without trial at the Curragh in the 1940s.

Also that year he gave the oration in St Coman's Cemetery, Roscommon town when his Quartermaster on the Staff of the Second Western, Joe McDevitt of Kilcar, Co. Donegal was buried. He praised Joe as a gifted person who had been a teacher on the staff of Pearse's school, St Enda's in Rathfarnham, Dublin.

SOLE FAITHFUL SURVIVOR
IN 1969 AND 1986

THE FOLLOWING YEAR, 1969, was notable in Tom Maguire's career. He was by now the sole faithful survivor of the Second (All-Ireland) Dáil. His comrades had all passed on: Mary Mac Swiney in 1942, Professor Stockley in 1943 and Count Plunkett, at the remarkable age of 97 in 1948. Seán Ó Ceallaigh (Sceilg) died in 1957, Cathal Ó Murchadha in 1958 and then Brian Ó hUiginn in 1963. Brian, the last to go with the exception of Tom himself, had always been a close friend. He had brought out the *Wolfe Tone Annual* for 30 years from 1932 to 1962 and also published Celtic-style Christmas cards each year. He edited the *Wolfe Tone Weekly* – successor to the suppressed *An Phoblacht* – from 1937 to 1939 until it in turn was banned north and south.

On January 21, 1969, the 50th anniversary of the First Dáil, Tom spoke in the Oak Room of the Dublin Mansion House. He was now the last living link who stood faithful to the revolutionary First and Second Dáil. At the end of that year on December 31, Tom Maguire issued a formal statement to the news media.[20]

Following a split in the Republican Movement that month he disowned the Officials who had accepted the

General Maguire adopts a firing position with a Lee Enfield service rifle captured from the British forces in the Tourmakeady ambush. He is pictured with Ruairí Ó Brádaigh at Easter, 1987, when General Maguire was aged 95.

Leinster House, Stormont and Westminster parliaments. He recognised the Provisional Army Council of the IRA as the legitimate successor to the 1938 body. The Army Convention that month had "neither the right nor the authority" to pass a resolution recognising the British and the two partition parliaments," Maguire declared.

By September 1970 the Provisionals had re-organised the country and held a regular General Army Convention that month. Tom Maguire attended, an imposing and erect figure with an obvious military presence. When he entered the hall the assembled delegates were brought to their feet and stood at attention by the chairman. He then exchanged salutes with Comdt-Gen Maguire and introduced him to the meeting.[21]

In his address the last faithful survivor told the Supreme Army Authority, as the IRA constitution defines an Army Convention, that the authority of the last sovereign parliament for all Ireland now rested with them. They should guard it, resisting all betrayals, and be true to their trust. In the coming eventful years they should strive to bring about the Third Dáil of the All-Ireland Republic to which as an Army they would give allegiance as required by the IRA Constitution.

With the development of the struggle in the Six Occupied Counties from 1969 the Irish population in England became involved. One of these, Frank Stagg from Hollymount, Co. Mayo died on hunger strike in Wakefield Prison, Yorkshire in February 1976 and Tom Maguire, still very sprightly at 84 years, agreed to give the funeral oration. Stagg's father, Henry had served under Tom Maguire in the South Mayo Brigade in the 1920s while his uncle Patrick Vahey of Ballinrobe was a Volunteer in the same Brigade who died in 1922 from the rigours of active service.

Frank Stagg's body was, however, seized by the Dublin government while en route by air from England and was buried in a new grave some distance from the Republican Plot in Leigue Cemetery, Ballina. Convoys of 26-County State troops in lorries and armoured cars made up the funeral while the Special Branch dug the grave. The family had boycotted this charade as had the general public.

It was in an atmosphere of tension next day that huge crowds of people from all over Ireland paraded to the Republican Plot in a symbolic funeral. Tom Maguire was

equal to the occasion and spoke in the presence of Stagg's mother, brothers and sisters while a great number of Special Branch and uniformed police surrounded the Plot. Large forces of the Free State army under arms with many in riot gear had taken up positions on the hills around the cemetery but nevertheless the great attendance enabled full military honours to be rendered to the latest to die for Ireland. Tom Maguire had once more played a central role on a memorable occasion.

Later in the 1970s he at last gave a full length interview to Uinseann Mac Eoin who included it in his book *Survivors*, published in 1980 and again in 1987 in a new and enlarged edition. His wife and comrade Christina Feeney also contributed to that interview. She died a few years later in January 1984 having stood shoulder to shoulder with Tom down all the years. Ar dheis Dé go raibh a hanam uasal.

Tom Maguire was by this time not only the last faithful survivor of the Second (All-Ireland) Dáil. He was now the sole survivor of "the Government of the Irish Republic which is Dáil Éireann" to quote from the Republican Oath

This was the occasion of the unveiling of a memorial plaque on the site of the old Tuam Workhouse, at the spot where six Volunteers of General Maguire's command were executed by the Free State in 1923. This was the last occasion on which Tom Maguire spoke in public, April 21, 1985.

General Maguire congratulating Fianna Éireann. In the background are Veterans of the Second Western Division, IRA: (left to right) Jimmy Cleary, Athenry, Galway; John Walshe, Robeen, Hollymount, Sth Mayo; Sonny O'Donnell, Claran, Headford, North Galway; John Snee, Kilkelly, East Mayo.

of Allegiance of 1919. Tom made his last public appearance in April 1985 when he unveiled a memorial plaque at the spot on the old Tuam Workhouse site where six IRA Volunteers were executed by Free State firing squad 62 years earlier.[22] His brother Seán was one of these.

Comdt-General Maguire first inspected a Guard of Honour of veterans of the Second Western Division, IRA drawn up in front of the place of execution. The *Western People* newspaper of Ballina, Co. Mayo carried a photograph of this historic inspection by the late General Officer Commanding the Division on its front page.

Tom's brief address on that day is recorded: "The Republican soldiers who died here and their comrades in Athlone fell before Free State firing squads. They were all attached to the Second Western Division which I commanded. They were my men and their blood was spilt by those who were unfit. They gave their lives for the All-Ireland Republic then under attack. That Republic was overthrown and has yet to be restored."

"They were my men," General Maguire repeated, "and they were faithful. They were faithful to their oath to defend the Republic against all enemies, foreign and domestic. Others were unfaithful, were unworthy."

He then quoted from Pearse's poem dedicated to his

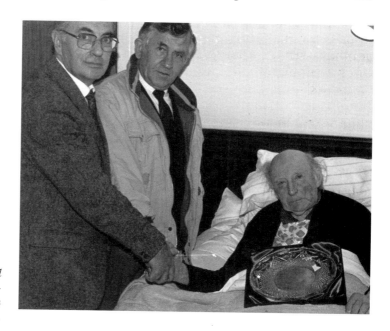

Ruairí Ó Brádaigh, Roscommon and Dan Hoban, Mayo, making a presentation to General Maguire on the occasion of his 100th birthday, March 28, 1992.

[Handwritten autograph in Irish, signed] Tomás MacUidhir, Comdt General, Late G. O. C. 2nd Western Division Óglaigh na hEireann & R A, Teachta Dála an Dara Dáil Éireann 1921 — 17th December 1984

Autograph on the book Survivors.

mother: "My sons were faithful and they fought." In conclusion he said it was good that such sacrifices were commemorated but they must also remember that their objective remained unattained. He was proud to be associated with that day's worthy ceremony.

Eighteen months later came yet another crisis in the Republican Movement: after seventeen years of heroic struggle against British Forces an IRA Convention again accepted the 26-County parliament and state. Tom Maguire, now 94 years, met the situation head-on as usual. On October 22, 1986[23] he issued another public statement. He said he spoke as the sole surviving Teachta Dála of the Second Dáil Éireann and as the sole survivor of the Executive Council of that All-Ireland Dáil.

He had, he said, recognised the Provisional Army Council in December 1969. Now in 1986 he stated:

"I do not recognise the legitimacy of any Army Council styling itself the Council of the Irish Republican Army which lends support to any person or organisation styling itself Sinn Féin and prepared to enter the partition parliament of Leinster House."

There was no difference between entering the partition parliament of Leinster House and entering a partition parliament of Stormont, he continued. "The majority of delegates to a recent IRA Convention purported to accept the Leinster House partition parliament, and in doing so broke faith and betrayed the trust placed in their predecessors in 1969," he went on.

Maguire concluded with a quotation from Terence Mac Swiney's *Principles of Freedom*: "If but a few are faithful found, they must be all the more steadfast for being but a few." About that time he gave an interview to Michael Finlan of the *Irish Times* which was carried in that newspaper.

With the continuation of the political organisation of the Movement as Republican Sinn Féin and that organisation's re-dedication to the principles of Irish Republicanism, Tom Maguire consented to become Patron on the occasion of the 83rd Ard-Fheis in October 1987. Thereafter he sent messages of encouragement to succeeding Ard-Fheiseanna and took a keen interest in matters Republican.

In September 1987 Tom Maguire and Michael Flannery of New York met at Tom's home in Cross and had a discussion lasting two-and-a-half hours. Flannery had been active with the North Tipperary Brigade IRA from 1916 to 1925 when he went to the United States. There he was to the fore in supporting the Irish revolutionary movement to the end of his days in 1994.

In his Ard-Fheis Address that year Ruairí Ó Brádaigh, Uachtarán, Sinn Féin Poblachtach, said: "It was a proud moment for those present when Michael Flannery and General Tom Maguire met in support of Republican Sinn Féin in 1987 – the one the living link with the revolutionary All-Ireland Dáil of 1919-22 and the other the pillar of support from Irish-America for over 60 years".

On the 70th anniversary of the suppression of the First (All-Ireland) Dáil by the British government, September 10, 1989 Tom took part in the making of an historic video which included an important interview with journalist and political commentator Nollaig Ó Gadhra. In January, 1990 his home at Cross in South Mayo – which had been burned by British Forces following the Tourmakeady Ambush – was the inspirational starting point for a march across

Ruairí Ó Brádaigh and Councillor Frank Glynn presenting a copy of An Chéad Dáil Éireann agus an Ghaeilge *by Nollaig Ó Gadhra to Tom Maguire on the 70th anniversary of the suppression of the First (All-Ireland) Dáil by the British Cabinet on September 10, 1919. A video record of the presentation and of an interview with General Maguire was made on the same occasion, September 10, 1989.*

Ireland via Galway and Athlone to Dublin. The march demanded All-Ireland democracy and greater local democracy as it moved to the capital in stages. Its arrival there coincided with the anniversary of the First Dáil on January 21.

On March 28, 1992 Tom Maguire entered his second century, still reading the newspapers and keeping a lively interest in national affairs. Messages of congratulations poured in to him at his son's home from all over Ireland, from Britain, the US and Canada, from South Africa and Australia. Congressman Benjamin Gilman read a message of congratulations into the official record of the United States House of Representatives in Washington DC.

An official Republican Sinn Féin group led by Ruairí Ó Brádaigh, Uachtarán, visited him and made him a presentation. The video made in 1989 was shown at a press conference in a Castlebar hotel while national and local papers gave space to mark the occasion. The *Irish Press* noted that he refused to accept the usual £250 cheque on reaching 100 years from the President of the 26-County State.

Tom did not wish to be offensive: there was nothing personal in his action, he said; he just did not recognise the office. Tom Maguire was fittingly honoured at home and abroad as a fearless Republican soldier and as an Irish public representative of a great generation. None could deny that he had remained unswervingly true to his solemn Oath of Allegiance to the All-Ireland Republic. Tom's story was that of the Republican struggle in the twentieth century.

The following year in an article to mark his 101st birthday, *SAOIRSE – Irish Freedom* observed that he was "still bearing up despite his great age". In a tribute published in the Irish Post (London) columnist Frank Dolan concluded a survey of Tom Maguire's career and principles thus:

"The rest is history. Generations have passed. Even [Provisional] Sinn Féin led by Gerry Adams now recognises the twenty-six-county Dáil. But not Commandant-General Tom Maguire and the small but still vocal Republican Sinn Féin led by Ruairí Ó Brádaigh.

"All very complex and academic, you may say. Still that is how it is and it derives from that uncompromising 'Fenian faith' exemplified by such as O'Donovan Rossa and Tom Clarke. It's not politics and it's out of kilter with the overwhelming mass of Nationalist opinion of all colours and shades. But Tom Maguire will insist that there is only one colour – an unfading green."

Just over three months later on July 5, 1993 came the end. The victor of Kilfall and Tourmakeady, the last and faithful Deputy of the Second (All-Ireland) Dáil breathed his last at the home of his son, Dr Seán Maguire in Castlebar, Co. Mayo. His funeral on July 7 to Cross Cemetery where he lies beside his wife and comrade Christina was an appropriate tribute to a life lived for Ireland and her freedom.

Two Veterans in discussion in September, 1987. Michael Flannery, New York, USA, formerly of North Tipperary Brigade, IRA, makes a point to Tom Maguire.

On January 21, 1994 – just six months later – a fitting ceremony took place at the graveside of Tom Maguire. The date was auspicious, the 75th anniversary of the inaugural meeting of the First (All-Ireland) Dáil. *SAOIRSE*[24] reported in its February edition under the heading "Final salute to Comdt-General Tom Maguire" that the true IRA had paid full military honours.

It carried a statement from the Irish Republican Publicity Bureau signed B Ó Ruairc, Rúnaí, stating that "a firing-party of Volunteers of Óglaigh na hÉireann – the Irish Republican Army – loyal to the principles of the late Comdt-General Tom Maguire rendered military honours at his grave in Cross, Co. Mayo." The statement noted that as well as being the last survivor of the Second (All-Ireland) Dáil he was also the last general officer of the Irish Republican Army of 1921.

Two photos were carried: one showed a firing-party of young men with rifles wearing black berets. The other was a picture of the men presenting arms at the graveside while the Volunteer in charge gave a military salute.

The torch which had been held aloft for so long had been passed on.

Dílis go hÉag.

Addendum
Last political will and testament

Two-and-a-half years after Tom Maguire's death, in February 1996, *SAOIRSE* carried the text of what has become known as "Tom Maguire's last political will and testament". This book was being prepared for publication at the time and the circulation of the "will" was in time for it to be included here as an addendum.

SAOIRSE reported that it had received a press release dated January 12, 1996 from the Irish Republican Publicity Bureau, signed B Ó Ruairc, Rúnaí.

It contained a statement of recognition by Comdt-General Thomas Maguire of the Continuity Executive and the Continuity Army Council as the lawful leadership of the Irish Republican Army and a declaration that "the governmental authority delegated in the Proclamation of 1938 now resides in the Continuity Army Council and its lawful successors".

Easter 1987
General Maguire, along with Seán Keenan, Derry, Liam Murray, Belfast and Caoimhín Mac Cathmhaoil, Galway; and (back) Bob Murray, Belfast and Peter Farley, New Jersey, USA.

The full text is given on another page.[25] It was signed by Comdt-General Maguire in the presence of two witnesses[26] and dated July 25, 1987. Another stone had been put into place on the rocky road to Irish freedom.

Críoch

IARFHOCAL

LOOKING BACK NOW 80 years after the Rising of 1916 and the First Dáil of 1919, it is relevant to ask "How does she stand?" Where are we now and what has happened?

In summary, defection after defection took place from the ranks of the Republican Movement. Fianna Fáil followed on Cumann na nGaedheal (Fine Gael), to be joined by Clann na Poblachta, the Workers' Party, Democratic Left and the Provisionals. In all cases the 26-County State was strengthened and the Movement weakened.

Most of these parties went on to become "England's policemen in Ireland", collaborating fully with British rule in the Six Occupied Counties, using the firing squad and the British hangman and the concentration camp against Republicans, allowing them to die on hunger strike and even extraditing political prisoners – handing them over to the British Forces.

Since 1922 the Republican Movement in its efforts for Irish Freedom has been opposed both by the British government and the 26-County State. Were it not for the collaboration of the latter, the Movement would have won through long since.

If at any stage he had accepted the Free State – England's alternative to Irish independence – Tom Maguire could have enjoyed the fruits of office. Cumann na nGaedheal (Fine Gael), Fianna Fáil and Clann na Poblachta all sought him. With his great ability and his national record he could have done well for himself in material terms.

Instead, he adhered to his oath to the All-Ireland Republic, set an example to the youth of succeeding generations and maintained his integrity and honour to the ripe old age of 101. To the very end the Movement had but to call on his assistance.

He worked hard, raised a family which are a credit to him and was beholden to no Leinster House political party. He remained an inspiration and an example of unselfish service to Ireland and the Irish people. He would not be bought, could not be broken or bent.

Ireland today remains partitioned into two British-imposed statelets. The Six-County nationalist population has been abandoned since 1922 and the Unionist Veto on the future of Ireland is accepted widely on all sides. The effect of this is that 18% of the population of Ireland continues to dictate the future to the remaining 82%. Indeed a regular columnist in the *Irish Times*, Vincent Browne on June 5, 1996 noted:

"At the core of Irish nationalism was the 'principle' that the Irish people as a whole had the right to self-determination. Through the benign agency of Humespeak, this principle has been abandoned entirely.

"Humespeak has introduced the nonsensical idea that there can be national self-determination without there being national self-determination – i.e. that there has to be agreement on how national self-determination is to be exercised.

"And the [Provisional] Sinn Féin opposition to this remains temporary and tactical, for in agreeing to join in what unionists derisively call 'the pan-nationalist alliance' they are joining with those who have abandoned nationalism."

With the loss of high ideals has come a general lowering of standards in public life as scandal succeeds scandal. With the backing down on the nationalist position, the Irish language and even our neutrality, has come the stark reality that one out of every two people born in Ireland since 1922 has been forced to emigrate.

It has become fashionable to decry the small wars of national liberation as peoples struggle to regain their place on the face of the earth. At the same time the very same public commentators push for the abandonment of neutrality and for membership of military blocs with nuclear weapons. They cannot wait to join with the big powers in "the resource wars of the 21st century" (Jacques Delors), even though the great majority of casualties in modern wars are civilian rather than military.

The environment is polluted in the interests of a rampant and often multi-national capitalism while a drugs culture spreads, unemployment is at an all-time high and crime abounds.

One consistent strain running through all of this is the world-wide loss of morality – a sense of right and wrong – including political morality. The pernicious doctrine that "there is no principle except to win" prevails on all sides while the exploitation of humankind by their fellows continues. Man-made famines exist in the midst of plenty.

It is all a far cry from the ideals that men and women such as Tom Maguire espoused to their cost all their lives. But the end is not yet. In Ireland and among Irish exiles there is a growing acceptance that Republican Sinn Féin's analysis is correct, that the current "process" is simply a ploy to gain another 50 or 75 years of life for the Six-County colonial statelet which was tottering up to a decade ago.

A new and updated Stormont with cross-border boards lies at the end of this process with British rule copperfastened for the foreseeable future. The alternative is what Tom Maguire and his comrades spent their lives striving for – complete British disengagement from Ireland and the right of the Irish people acting as a unit freely to determine their own future.

The modern expression of that is advocated by the organisation of which Tom Maguire was Patron to the day of his death. Their programme is Ireland of the four provinces, including a nine-county Ulster, with maximum devolution of power and decision-making to the lowest level.

Republican Sinn Féin, strong in its ideology, gains confidence and strength as it progresses. Tom Maguire would be happy at that.

Terence Mac Swiney, the hunger-striker and martyred Lord Mayor of Cork, has written and Tom Maguire often quoted him: "If but a few are faithful found, they must be all the more steadfast for being but a few."

Choinnigh Tomás Mag Uidhir creideamh na bhFíníní. Bhí sé diongbháilte ina phrionsabail ach bhí so-lúbthacht an trodaire ann san am céanna. He was steadfast but with the flexibility of a fighter.

Beannacht Dé lena anam dílis cróga.

NOTES

1   *With the IRA in the Fight for Freedom – 1919 to the Truce*, page 211.
2   *ibid*.
3   Recounted in video made in 1989.
4   *The Singing Flame* (1978).
5   *Wolfe Tone Annual*, 1962.
6   *The Singing Flame*, page 51.
7   Dorothy Macardle: *The Irish Republic*, page 713.
8   Official report, Parliamentary Debates, Provisional Parliament, September 9, 1922.
9   Brian P Murphy: *Patrick Pearse and the Lost Republican Ideal* (1991).
10 Dr Crowley, North Mayo; David R Kent, East Cork; Caitlín Brugha, Waterford; Austin Stack, Kerry; Oscar Traynor, North Dublin; and the two Independent Republicans: Art Ó Cléirigh, NUI and Daniel Corkery, North Cork.
11 Seán Cronin: *The McGarrity Papers* (1972), page 202.
12 *Survivors*, (1980).
13 Presidential Address of Seán Ó Ceallaigh (Sceilg) to Ard-Fheis of Sinn Féin, 1931, page 14.
14 Waterford; Co Dublin; Nth Mayo; Sligo-Leitrim; West Cork.
15 Tom Mitchell, Mid-Ulster; Philip Clarke, Fermanagh-South Tyrone; Ruairí Ó Brádaigh, Longford-Westmeath; John J. McGirl, Sligo-Leitrim; Eighneachán Ó hAnluain, Monaghan; John J. Rice, South Kerry.
16 Sylvester Fitzsimons, Co. Roscommon.
17 *Wolfe Tone Weekly* December 17, 1938; see also *Irish Nationalism* by Seán Cronin (1980), pages 326-328.
18 Brian P. Murphy: *Patrick Pearse and the Lost Republican Ideal* (1991).
19 *An tÉireannach Aontuithe*, September 1952.
20 Text of statement issued by Comdt-Gen Tom Maguire on December 31, 1969.
21 Interview with author, 1980.
22 *Eleven Galway Martyrs*, 1985.
23 Text of statement issued by Comdt-Gen Maguire, October 22, 1986.
24 Photographs and copy of article.
25 See Appendix.
26 Interview with author, 1988.

APPENDICES

Dr Seán Maguire's recollections

Dr Maguire, son of Tom Maguire, now lives in Castlebar. He was born on December 16, 1925 and in 1996 he makes many interesting points.

Michael Martyn BE who was captured with Tom Maguire in 1922 was later Chief Assistant Co Engineer with Galway Co Council.

George Maguire of Claremorris, Tom's election agent in 1923, was a medical doctor. He was MO to the Second Western Division, appointed by my father. He had served in France in WWI with his brother who was killed there.

The uniforms of the Maguire brothers were used in the foiled raid on the RIC Barracks at Cross in 1920.

Art O'Connor was a lawyer, a barrister I believe. Elected in 1918 for South Kildare and again in 1921 as Sinn Féin Deputy for Kildare-Wicklow, he was appointed Minister for Agriculture in August of that year. He resigned as President of the Republic in December 1927 because he was going to practise in the Free State courts.

Joe McDevitt left Maynooth College to join the fight for freedom. He was later a prisoner in Edinburgh Jail where he was confined with criminals and prisoners serving life sentences for murder. While there he kept a diary written in Greek. Years later my mother returned it to him when he visited Cross.

Mary Mac Swiney's papers, including her constitution adopted by the Second Dáil in 1929, are in the Archives in University College, Dublin.

At the time of his capture in a dugout by Free State forces in 1922, my father had a revolver with him. He hid it in a hole in the wall. He did not surrender his gun EVER. Perhaps it was because the revolver was not found that he was not executed?

He started work with the Irish National Insurance Company and became an inspector with them. I think that was in 1929. Later, about the time of WWII he started as an insurance broker.

In Brian O'Higgins's Wolfe Tone Annual in the 1940s and 1950s his advertisement was carried: "Insurance. Fire, Motor, Accident and all classes of insurance arranged. Life Assurance a special feature. Tom Maguire, Insurance Broker, Cross, Claremorris, Co. Mayo." Brian O'Higgins was a particular friend of his.

My father was elected unopposed to the Second Dáil. The convention was held in Claremorris in May 1921. Conor Maguire, Claremorris, later Chief Justice in the 26 Counties, Coyne (I think his name was William), later a District Justice in South Mayo and James MacGarry, Claremorris were the candidates. Conor Maguire was nominated.

The first meeting of the Second Dáil Éireann, held in the Mansion House, Dublin on August 16, 1921. Tom Maguire was among the Teachtaí present.

Later, the meeting was breaking up when somebody – we don't know the name – said: "What about the man that is wounded on the mountain?" Conor Maguire withdrew. My father was adopted. Dr George Maguire, Claremorris, Conor's brother who was to be Conor's election agent volunteered to act in that capacity for my father. He continued to be my father's election agent in subsequent elections.

There was a contest in the East Mayo constituency, which included the Ballaghaderreen area of Co. Roscommon, in the 1918 general election. Trouble was expected from the Dillon (Parliamentary Party) faction. A contingent of Volunteers came from Clare under Comdt Peadar O'Loughlin to "police" the election.

My father and a group of Mayo Volunteers joined O'Loughlin and his men. They marched from Charlestown to Ballaghaderreen during the election equipped with pick-axe handles.

(South Mayo and Clare East and West were three of the 24 constituencies where Sinn Féin candidates were returned unopposed in 1918. Election workers from these areas were free then to participate in contests elsewhere. – Editor)

Peadar O'Loughlin died on active service in August 1922. He was a diabetic. Martin Devitt of Ennistymon, Co Clare was a comrade of his who was killed in action against British forces in February 1920. My father unveiled a memorial to them in Neughaville, near Kilfenora.

I myself have a clear recollection of the dwelling house and farmyard in Cross being raided by [Free State] police. One of them was

Christine Maguire, wife of Tom Maguire

named Hernon. When I came to live in Castlebar he approached me and offered to sell me his house! We were never raided after Fianna Fáil came into office in the 26 Counties.

In the Blueshirt time there was a big meeting in Castlebar addressed by O'Duffy. A group from Headford, Shrule and Glencorrrib attended it on horseback. On their way home they stopped in Cross to augment the "refreshments" they had already taken.

Fortified with Dutch courage they began to shout and taunt: "Where is Maguire now?" I remember quite clearly my father walking up the bridge, as we say, and right to the south end of the village and back down again. There was total silence.

I clearly remember he had his right hand in his jacket pocket. Years later he told me what was in his pocket! I asked him what would have happened if he had used it? He said: "What could they do but give me a few months in jail..?"

TOURMAKEADY
Third of May 1921

(Air: The Boys from the County Cork)

"We're off to Tourmakeady, boys,"
Our leader then did say,
"For another blow to crush the foe
And clear them far away."

When first we skirted the Partry hills
'Twas early in the spring
And round the mountains far and wide
We formed in a ring.

The English were determined
That O'Brien should never fight,
And every day throughout that year
They searched for him far and wide.

He first tested his mettle
At the battle of Port Royal,
When the South Mayo Flying Column
Fought to reverse the English smile.

"Hands up!" cried Captain Emmerson
But he proudly answered "No",
And he fell for Irish freedom
As he blazed the Saxon foe.

We lost one man, God rest his soul,
From earth he passed away;
He was a noble soldier
Of the famous IRA.

His name was Michael O'Brien
From the parish of the Neale.
The Lord have mercy on his soul
And grant old Ireland freedom.

We gained that day in victory,
And left them lying low
And we let them know we're the IRA
From the County of Mayo.

These lines were collected from Pat O'Brien (born 1909), Sléibhín, Roscommon town, formerly a CIE railway man of Cregmore, Kilmaine, Co. Mayo. His brother Terence, a member of the South Mayo Flying Column (see photograph), took part in the Tourmakeady Ambush. Pat O'Brien got the song from Patrick Walsh, an old man of the same townland as himself, in 1926 or '27.
South Mayo Volunteers used to shelter in Walsh's home while on active service against the Free State Army in 1922-23. They composed the song and gave it to him. Many of the same Volunteers had seen service at Tourmakeady on May 3, 1921.

SAOIRSE ÉIREANN

WOLFE TONE WEEKLY

Vol. 2. No. 16.   SATURDAY, DECEMBER 17th, 1938   Twopence.

I. R. A. TAKE OVER THE GOVERNMENT OF THE REPUBLIC

ONE of the most memorable events of our time took place on December 8, the anniversary of the Four Martyrs, when the Government of the Republic of Ireland was taken over from the Executive Council of Dail Eireann by the Council of the Irish Republican Army:

This was done, as the official announcement given below states, in the spirit of a decision taken by the First Dail Eireann at the height of the War of Independence, when it seemed that enemy action would sweep into prison all, or nearly all, the elected representatives of the people.

The official announcement released for publication to-day is as follows :—

DÁIL ÉIREANN

De ḃriġ go ndearna arm Sacsan Poblaċt Éireann d'ionsuiḋe agus d'aṫ-ionsuiḋe agus go ndearna mór-ċuid de ṫeaċtaiḃ an Ṗobail a tréigean ó deireaḋ for-fógraḋ na Poblaċta um Cáisc a 1916 do deiṁniugaḋ ag Tionól Tosnuiġṫe Dála Éireann trí bliaḋna d'a éis, deiṁimíd-ne tré'n scríḃinn seo an t-ugdarás a tugaḋ dúinn do ċur fé ḃrágaid Comairle an Airm mar is dual dúinn do réir mar d'órduig Dáil Éireann um earraċ a 1921, is mar d'órduig an Dara Dáil i ndráṫ.

Agus sinn ag cur an dualgais a bí mar ċúram oirṅg orainn le fiċe bliaḋan fá malairt comairce, molaimíd go fonnṁar do ṁuinntir na Poblaċta cois baile agus d'á cáirdiḃ uile i gcéin iad féin do deiġilt glan ó'n aċrann a bíos mar síor ċúram ar Riagaltas Sacsan; agus comairligmíd dóiḃ ó ċroiḋe gan aon spéis do ċur i sna tuartaiḃ cogaiḋ atá d'á leaṫaḋ ag Sacsaiḃ. Óir is ró-léir gur luga baoġal an náisiúin ársa so do ṫarraċ isteaċ i gcogaḋ, agus an fairrge mór mar teórainn aici, 'ná na náisiúin beaga atá i n-a luiġe idir Sacsaiḃ is an tír gur mian le Riagaltas Sacsan a basgaḋ.

Tá dóċas croiḋe againn agus sinn ag leagaḋ ar sciṁam oiriġ ar Arm na Poblaċta go mbeiḋ dílse is meanma ár marṫar mar réalt eolais aca i ngaċ céim d'á gcuirfid díoḃ is iad ag lorg saoirse Éireann; ar an intinn sin craobscaoiltear an t-ugdarás so fó láṁaiḃ Árd-Comairle Dála Éireann .i. Riagaltas na Poblaċta.

Seán Ua Ceallaiġ, Ceann Comairle.

Seoirse Noble Cont	Máire Nic Suibne
Ua Pluinnscéid	Uilliam F. P. Stoclaiġ
Brian Ó hUiginn	
Caṫal Ó Murċaḋa	Tomás MacGuidir

Baile Áṫa Cliaṫ, an t-oċtmaḋ lá de mí na Nodlag a 1938.

(TRANSLATION)

DÁIL ÉIREANN

IN consequence of armed opposition ordered and sustained by England, and the defection of elected representatives of the people over the period since the Republican Proclamation of Easter 1916 was ratified, three years later, by the newly inaugurated Government of the Irish Republic, we hereby delegate the authority reposed in us to the Army Council, in the spirit of the decision taken by Dail Eireann in the Spring of 1921, and later endorsed by the Second Dail.

In thus transferring the trust of which it has been our privilege to be the custodians for twenty years, we earnestly exhort all citizens and friends of the Irish Republic at home and abroad to dissociate themselves openly and absolutely from England's unending aggressions; and we urge on them utterly to disregard England's recurring war scares, remembering that our ancient and insular nation, bounded entirely by the seas, has infinitely less reason to become involved in the conflicts now so much threatened than have the neutral small nations lying between England and the Power she desires to overthrow.

Confident, in delegating this sacred trust to the Army of the Republic that, in their every action towards its consummation, they will be inspired by the high ideals and the chivalry of our martyred comrades, we, as Executive Council of Dail Eireann, Government of the Republic, append our names.

Seán Ua Ceallaiġ, Ceann Comairle.

Seoirse Noble Cont	Máire Nic Suibne
Ua Pluinnscéid	Uilliam F. P. Stoclaiġ
Brian Ó hUiginn	
Caṫal Ó Murċaḋa	Tomás MacGuidir

Dublin, December 8, 1938.

Comdt. General Thomas Maguire's Statement of 1969

We publish in full the text of a statement issued by Comdt. General Thomas Maguire, Cross, Co. Mayo, on the question of Republican leadership:

An IRA convention, held in December, 1969, by a majority of the delegates attending, passed a resolution removing all embargoes on political participation in parliament from the Constitution and Rules of the IRA.

Powers Delegated in 1938

The effect of the resolution is the abandonment of what is popularly termed the "Abstentionist Policy". The "Abstentionist Policy" means that Republican candidates contesting parliamentary elections in Leinster House, Stormont or Westminster give pre-election pledges not to take seats in any of those parliaments. The Republican candidates seek election to the 32-county Parliament of the Irish Republic, the Republican Dáil or Dáil Éireann, to give it its official title. The declared objective is to elect sufficient representatives to enable the 32-County Dáil Éireann to be re-assembled.

In December, 1938, the surviving faithful members of the latest 32-County Republican parliament, the Second Dáil, elected in 1921, delegated their executive powers of government to the Army Council of the IRA. This proclamation of 1938 was signed by S. S. Ó Ceallaigh (Sceilg), Ceann Comhairle, Mary Mac Swiney, Count Plunkett, Cathal Ó Murchú, Brian O'Higgins, Professor Stockley and myself, Tomás Maguire.

Neither right nor authority

The majority of the delegates at the December, 1969, IRA Convention, having passed the resolution referred to above, proceeded to elect an Executive which in turn appointed a new Army Council, committed to implement the resolution.

That Convention had neither the right nor the authority to pass such a resolution.

Accordingly, I, as the sole surviving member of the Executive of Dáil Éireann, and the sole surviving signatory of the 1938 Proclamation, hereby declare that the resolution is illegal and that the alleged Executive and Army Council are illegal, and have no right to claim the allegiance of either soldiers or citizens of the Irish Republic.

Provisional Army Council

The delegates who opposed the resolution, together with delegates from units which were not represented at the Convention, met subsequently in Convention and repudiated the resolution. They re-affirmed their allegiance to the Irish Republic and elected a Provisional Executive which in turn appointed a Provisional Army Council.

Lawful Executive and Council

I hereby further declare that the Provisional Executive and the Provisional Army Council are the lawful Executive and Army Council respectively of the IRA and that the governmental authority delegated in the Proclamation of 1938 now resides in the Provisional Army Council and its lawful successors. I fully endorse their call for support for Irish people everywhere towards the realisation of the full freedom of Ireland.

Dated the 31st day of December, 1969.

Signed: Thomas Maguire,
Comdt. Gen.
(Tomás Mac Uidhir).

Entering Leinster House
A Veteran Speaks, 1986

There is no difference between entering the partition parliament of Leinster House and entering a partition parliament of Stormont.

I speak as the sole surviving Teachta Dála of the Second Dáil Éireann and as the sole surviving member of the Executive of the Second Dáil Éireann.

In December, 1969, as the sole surviving member of the Executive of the Second Dáil Éireann, I recognised the Provisional Army Council, which remained true to the Irish Republic as the lawful Army of the Thirty-two County Irish Republic.

I do not recognise the legitimacy of any Army Council styling itself the Council of the Irish Republican Army which lends support to any person or organisation styling itself as Sinn Féin and prepared to enter the partition parliament of Leinster House.

The majority of delegates to a recent IRA convention purported to accept the Leinster House partition parliament, and in so doing broke faith and betrayed the trust placed in their predecessors in 1969.

The Irish Republic, proclaimed in arms in Easter Week 1916 and established by the democratic majority vote of the people in the General Election of 1918, has been defended by Irish Republicans for several generations. Many have laid down their lives in that defence. Many others have suffered imprisonment and torture.

I am confident that the Cause so nobly served will yet triumph.

"If but a few are faithful found, they must be all the more steadfast for being but a few"

(Terence Mac Swiney in *Principles of Freedom*)

Dated the 22nd day of October, 1986

Signed: Thomas Maguire
Tomás Maguidhir
Comdt. General

STATEMENT OF RECOGNITION
BY COMDT. GENERAL TOM MAGUIRE

A second statement from the Irish Republican Publicity Bureau was sent to *SAOIRSE*, dated January 12, 1996. It contains a statement of recognition of the Continuity Executive and Continuity Army Council by Comdt. General Thomas Maguire, which he made on July 25, 1987. It is effectively his last political will and testament. We publish it in full below:

'We have been asked to release the following statement from Comdt. General Thomas Maguire made by him before his death which occurred in 1993:

'Statement from Comdt. General Thomas Maguire

'I refer to my statement, dated 22nd day of October, 1986, and I speak again, as the sole surviving Teachta Dála of the Second Dáil Éireann, and the sole surviving member of the Executive of the Second Dáil.

'In that statement, I referred to my recognition in December, 1969, of the Provisional Army Council of the IRA, which had remained true to the Irish Republic, as the lawful Army of the Thirty Two County Irish Republic.

'I also stated on 22nd October, 1986, that I did not recognise the legitimacy of an Army Council, styling itself the Council of the Irish Republican Army, which lent support to any person or organisation styling itself Sinn Féin, and prepared to enter the partition parliament of Leinster House.

'I referred, as well, to the IRA Convention, which had taken place shortly before the 22nd October, 1986. The Executive of the IRA had, by a majority, opposed entering Leinster House. The faithful members of that Executive, in accordance with the IRA Constitution, filled the vacancies in the Executive, and that Executive continues as the lawful Executive of the Irish Republican Army. The Continuity Executive has appointed an Army Council of the IRA.

'I quote the following extract from my statement of 31st December 1969:

'In December, 1938, the surviving faithful members of the latest 32 County Republican Parliament, the Second Dáil elected in 1921, delegated their executive powers of government to the Army Council of the IRA. This Proclamation of 1938 was signed by S. S. Ó Ceallaigh (Sceilg), Ceann Comhairle, Mary Mac Swiney, Count Plunkett, Cathal Ó Murchú, Brian O'Higgins, Professor Stockley and myself, Tomás Maguire'.

'I hereby declare that the Continuity Executive and the Continuity Army Council are the lawful Executive and Army Council respectively of the Irish Republican Army, and that the governmental authority, delegated in the Proclamation of 1938, now resides in the Continuity Army Council, and its lawful successors.

'Dated the 25th day of July 1987
Signed: Thomas Maguire
Tomás Maguidhir
Comdt. General.'

Congressional Record

House of Representatives

COMMANDANT GENERAL TOM
MAGUIRE, T.D.

Hon. Benjamin A. Gilman
of New York

IN THE HOUSE OF REPRESENTATIVES

Wednesday, July 22, 1992

Mr. Gilman. Mr. Speaker, I rise to take this opportunity to recognise an extraordinary man on the occasion of his 100th birthday. On march 28, 1992, Commandant Gen. Maguire, the sole surviving member of the 2nd Dail Eireann – the first Irish parliament, elected after the 1919 Irish declaration of Independence – began his second century. This is an event of great significance among the Irish Diaspora as well as the people of Ireland.

In Ireland the President recognizes such events with a personal message and a check. When the individual who reaches the century mark is also a national hero, a former combat leader, and a former national legislator, the occasion should attract the attention of every legislative body.

Tom Maguire is respected by Irish people throughout the world, and in particular by those with connections to County Mayo, as a man who sought peace with justice and honor for all of Ireland. Commandant Gen. Maguire, T.D., a soldier and patriot, symobolizes those whose sacrifices and steadfast devotion led to the creation of the modern Irish State.

In recognition of the 100th birthday of Commandant Gen. Tom Maguire sole surviving member of the 2nd Dail Eireann, I invite my colleagues to pause in its deliberation to congratulate Commandant General Maguire, T.D., for a life of steadfast devotion to the cause of liberty and justice for all, and for peace with justice and honor for all Ireland. May he be remembered with the company of those brave men and women who served in the defence of the Irish republic proclaimed during Easter Week, 1916.

The printed program book of the 1991 New York Saint Patrick's Day parade, the largest parade in the world, contained a retrospective article on Commandant Gen. Tom Maguire, T.D., written by an Irish Immigrant from County Mayo, whose grandfather, Richard Cawley, native of Shrule, County Mayo, had served under Tom Maguire in the Irish war of independence(1919-1921) and who still vividly remembers Maguire's qualities of leadership. Gerald O'Hara, the author, is a native of Charlestown, County Mayo, and is also active in the Irish immigration reform movement. Additionally, he serves as a corporal in the 9th Regiment of the New York Guard. He now lives in New York with his wife Catherine.

Mr. Speaker, I request that the full text of the article entitled "Remember 1916" appear at this point in the Congressional Record.

REMEMBERING 1916

TOM MAGUIRE, COMMANDANT GENERAL, I.R.A. (SECOND DIVISION)

Born in Cross, South Mayo in 1892, Tom Maguire was the fourth child of eleven in a large nationalist family. His ancestors fought against the Williamites at Aughrim in 1691, with Humbert in 1798 and were active in the Fenian movement in the 1800's.

Considering this lineage, it was no surprise that the young Maguire was politically aware and had a keen interest in military history. In 1913 he was a member of the Irish Volunteers and took the anti-Redmond side in the split of 1914.

Events beyond their control precluded the Mayo Volunteers from taking any active part in the rising of 1916. This monumental event in Irish history left an indelible mark on Tom Maguire. He has this to say:

"The Easter insurrection came to me like a bolt form the blue. I will never forget my exhilaration; it was a turning point in my life to think that Irish men were fighting England on the streets of Dublin. I thank God for seeing such a day."

Prominent in organizing the first company of the I.R.A. in South Mayo Tom Maguire's leadership turned untrained and unarmed volunteers into an effective fighting force that engaged and defeated the British in several actions, notably the Kilfall ambush and the Tourmakeady ambush.

Tourmakeady, with its subsequent rear guard fighting and retreat across the Partry Mountains, made Tom Maguire a legend in his own lifetime. Wounded six times, and his adjutant, Michael O'Brien, fatally wounded after rendering him aid, he was carried by his own men where they broke through an encirclement of hundreds of British troops.

The tragic Civil War period found him imprisoned under threat of execution and his younger brother, John, was executed in Tuam.

Commandant General Tom Maguire, soldier and patriot, the last surviving member of the Second Dail, and one of the brave few who gained Ireland its first measure of freedom in six hundred years.

The people of Ireland and of County Mayo will forever be in their debt.

Commandant General Tom Maguire lives with his son Dr. Sean Maguire, in Castlebar, County Mayo.

FUNERAL OF TOMÁS MAG UIDHIR

The last link with the Second Dáil Éireann – the last All-Ireland Parliament – was broken on July 5, 1993 with the death of Commandant General Tom Maguire in Castlebar, Co. Mayo. He was 101 years of age. The last person to hold the rank of Comdt-General in the Irish Republican Army, he was elected Sinn Féin TD for South Mayo/South Roscommon in May 1921 and was re-elected in August 1923. He was Patron of Republican Sinn Féin since 1987.

Tom Maguire passed away at the home in Saleen, Castlebar of his son Dr Seán Maguire and daughter-in-law Pauline who had cared for him throughout his final illness. He had lived in his own home beside the Cross River in Cross village, five miles outside Ballinrobe, until 1990.

An immediate tribute was paid by Republican Sinn Féin President, Ruairí Ó Brádaigh, who was a frequent visitor to the Maguire home over the years. He described Tom Maguire as "epitomising the unyielding Republican resistance to British interference in internal Irish affairs throughout the 20th century. He represented the continuity, as a faithful survivor, of the Second All-Ireland Dáil

General Maguire's funeral cortege passes through his native Cross, Co Mayo. His coffin was borne behind the hearse from the church to the cemetery.

Éireann which was never dissolved.

"He adhered to the very end to the fundamental Republican position of giving allegiance to the All-Ireland Republic of 1916 and of the First Dáil. A fluent Irish speaker, he was an inspiration to several generations of Republicans. He was a close friend and associate of Brian O'Higgins of the Wolfe Tone Annual, Count Plunkett, Mary MacSwiney and 'Sceilg' (J. J. O'Kelly)."

The historic nature of Tom Maguire's long life as a national figure was underlined again and again as the arrangements for his funeral, in accordance with his wishes and agreed beforehand with his family, proceeded.

RESPECTS

Republicans from all parts of the country travelled to the Maguire home in Castlebar on Tuesday, July 6 to pay their respects and sympathise with the family. General Maguire was predeceased by his wife Christina in 1984. Her brother, Volunteer Pádraic Feeney, was killed by British Crown Forces at Tourmakeady on May 3, 1921. As well as Dr Seán Maguire, he is survived by sons Tom (Galway), Louis (St Louis) and Frank (Florida), daughter Mary McMonagle (Dublin), and sister Mrs Bridie O'Toole (Portarlington).

General Maguire's remains were removed from his son's house in Castlebar at 6pm as a very large crowd waited outside.

A Republican colour-party dressed in white shirts, black slacks and black berets rendered military honours as the coffin was carried from the house and placed on two chairs outside the front door. Dr Seán Maguire led the attendance in a decade of the Rosary in Irish.

Piper Larry O'Dowd of Sligo played a lament as the coffin was then lifted and placed in the hearse, the two chairs having been knocked over in accordance with a West of Ireland custom symbolising the utter finality of the occasion. Meanwhile the colour-party with flags furled and draped in black stood rigidly at attention.

After escorting the cortege a short distance along the Ballinrobe road, the colour-party fell out and the funeral proceeded between the shores of Lough Mask and Lough Carra through Ballinrobe and into Cross village.

The church was packed to overflowing for the Removal, presided over by Fr Pat Breen, a native of Omagh, Co Tyrone.

He said he regretted very much never having met Tom Maguire who, he said, advocated and practised armed struggle against tyranny and foreign rule in his country. He quoted from the Book of Ecclesiastes:

All things have their season, and in their times all things pass under heaven. A time to be born and a time to die. A time to plant and a time to pluck up that which is planted. A time to kill, and a time to heal. A time to destroy and a time to build. A time to weep and a time to laugh. A time to mourn and a time to dance...

Paying tribute to Tom Maguire's steadfastness and courage he said he had gone to join Michael O'Brien, killed in action at Tourmakeady, as well as his men who were executed in Tuam and Athlone.

He then listed all eleven who faced the firing squad: Comdt Frank Cunnane (Kilcoona), Seán Maguire (Cross, brother of Tom), Seán Newell (Headford), Michael Monaghan (Headford), Martin Moylan (Annaghdown), Séamas Ó Máille (Uachtar Ard), Michael Walsh, Stephen Joyce, Martin Burke (all Caherlistrane), Thomas Hughes (Athlone) and Hubert Collins (Headford).

Fr Breen quoted General Maguire's words when he unveiled a memorial at their graves in the Republican Plot, Donaghpatrick, in North Galway, in August 1952: "The generation of young men today and the coming years would renew those national aspirations and continue to strive for their attainment, namely the unification of Republican Ireland.

YOUTH

"He appealed to the youth especially, to follow in the footsteps of those brave men and not to be led astray by the false promises of politicians and collaborators. It was no shame to the men buried there or in the hundreds of such graves all over Ireland that the attainment of an Irish Republic was still unfinished and that Six Counties remained occupied by the enemy. Those shackles must be broken if they were to be true to the memory of all those

The flag, specially designed by Dáithí Ó Conaill, which was draped on General Maguire's coffin. The design of an Easter Lily on a blue field is based on IRA Brigade and Battalion colours.

Pat O'Brien (left) of Ballinrobe and Roscommon, whose brother, Terence, fought with the South Mayo Flying Column and Dr Seán Maguire, Castlebar, eldest son of General Maguire.

generations who had died for Ireland."

The Requiem Mass the following day at 12 noon was attended by an even larger crowd with mourners arriving from as far away as Cork, Kerry, Wexford, Belfast and Dublin.

The overflow from the small village church was accommodated by chairs placed outside as 13 priests concelebrated Requiem Mass, led by Dr Brian P Murphy of Glenstal Abbey, Co Limerick (see homily below).

SPECIAL FLAG

The coffin was draped in a special flag, based on the designs of IRA flags of the past, with an Easter Lily on a blue background with the lettering "Arm Phoblacht na hÉireann". On top of the flag was pinned General Maguire's Sam Browne belt.

The funeral procession was led by two pipers and a Republican Guard of Honour which flanked the coffin as it was carried in turn by Republican comrades and neighbours of Tom Maguire through Cross village.

The cortege halted momentarily at the Maguire home before crossing the bridge and making its way the short distance up the hill to the local cemetery.

At the graveside the IRA flag was folded and presented to General Maguire's daughter-in-law Pauline. The Last Post and Reveille was sounded by two buglers after the coffin was lowered into the grave in the family plot where General Maguire's wife, Christina, rests.

Dan Hoban, Newport, chaired the graveside ceremony on behalf of Republican Sinn Féin. Wreaths were then laid on behalf of the Republican Movement, Republican Sinn Féin, Cumann na mBan, Mayo Republicans, Connacht Republicans, Dublin Comhairle Ceantair, and many others.

Dan Hoban recalled his own family connection with Tom Maguire, his mother having sheltered him in Newport when he was training IRA Volunteers in the 1920s. He introduced Caoimhín Mac Cathmhaoil, Gaillimh, who read The Grave of Ruairí by T. W. Rolleston about the Last High-King of Ireland, Rory O'Connor, who is buried in nearby Cong Abbey.

Republican Sinn Féin President, Ruairí Ó Brádaigh, then delivered the oration, in which he said:

"Is tromchúiseach an dualgas atá orainn inniu, cé go bhfuil brón inár gcroíthe an lá seo, tá bród thar cuimse orainn mar, a Thomáis, níor ghéill tú don namhaid. Bheirimid buíochas go Dhia ar an ré fhada a thug Sé duit ar an saol seo agus beidh tú mar réalt eolais romhainn san am atá le teacht.

"This was a day we hoped would never come. The man who was our inspiration and was an inspiration for succeeding generations, Tom Maguire, that man who personified Terence MacSwiney's dictum 'If but a few are faithful found they must be all the more steadfast for being but a few' has gone from us."

He recalled that Tom Maguire's Fermanagh ancestors had travelled to Mayo after the Battle of Aughrim and that Fermanagh was represented at the funeral. An ancestor of his in 1798 joined the United Irish and French forces and fought all the way from Castlebar to Ballinamuck in Co Longford and survived. Tom's own father was a Fenian and a Land Leaguer.

Outlining General Maguire's Republican career Ruairí Ó Brádaigh referred to his statement as GOC Second Western Division, IRA on July 4, 1922 when the Four Courts was attacked, on the orders of the British government, by the Free State army. The statement declared his, and his

Division's allegiance to the All-Ireland Republic, and their willingness to defend it from attack.

"It went on: 'We have right and principle on our side, and we have as our comrades men who would rather die than surrender our unquestionable right to absolute independence'.

"It was at all times a joy and a privilege to know Tom Maguire. Speaking to him I always felt i láthair na staire a bhí mé, I was there in the presence of living history, and trying to learn.

"He would point out, not far from his house, in prehistoric times, the First Battle of Moytura was fought. He would then refer to Cong Abbey where his predecessor, one may say, Rory O'Connor, the last Irish High King, lived out his declining years and was buried.

SYMBOL

"Is it not a strange irony that the symbol of All-Ireland sovereignty, 800 years ago, lived out his declining years in this part of Ireland, and that 800 years later that the last symbol of All-Ireland sovereignty in the person of Tom Maguire lived out the last days of his life here in Cross, not two-and-a-half miles from the abbey of Cong, until he went to Castlebar to be cared for by his devoted family?

"Dignity, integrity and loyalty were Tom Maguire's hallmarks. He was a soldier, a military man but he was not a mercenary or a professional soldier. He was a citizen soldier with a political objective in view and here at his graveside on this historic day we salute his eighty years' service to the All-Ireland Republic, from the day he joined the Volunteers in 1913 up to today, 1993.

STEPPING STONES

"He would teach as the lesson, there should be no stepping stones. They had a stepping stone in 1922 and he would outline the disasters that followed. No 'interim solutions' to give it its modern terminology. British withdrawal and the freedom of Ireland, that was Tom Maguire's national agenda.

"He would point out the consequences of these half-baked solutions and say that the first thing it would do would be to divide the Movement. Then one half of the Movement would repress the other half at the enemy's behest and those who won their stepping stone would stagnate and grow to love it and the dynamic force for forward movement would be missing.

"He would then quote the words of Liam Mellows, speaking to those looking for an interim solution in 1922. Mellows said: 'Who will tell the British government when the time has come to tell it, to keep its hands off? Men will get into positions, men will hold power and men who get into positions and hold power will desire to remain undisturbed and will not want to be removed or will not take a step that will mean removal in the case of failure'.

TESTAMENT

"Tom Maguire's last political will and testament has not yet been published. Suffice it to say that he agreed with Pádraig Pearse: 'Until the English are at last beaten, the Irish have a duty to put a body of people on guard for the nation and it will be necessary for a band of the Irish to man the gap of danger'.

"Tom Maguire was most fulsome in his praise of the women in the Movement, saying that they were indeed the most loyal, and in particular he spoke of the intellectual Mary MacSwiney.

"He was always interested in the youth and their activities and wished to get regular reports on their progress. On his 100th birthday he asked to speak to representatives of them in private where he could give them encouragement.

"People of Mayo and indeed of all parts of Ireland we here today are grateful to God in his inscrutable wisdom for the long life he gave to our comrade Tom Maguire; for the devoted family he gave him; for his wife and lifelong comrade Christina; for Dr Seán Maguire, his wife Pauline and family who stand high in our estimation and gratitude for the care and loving devotion that they showered on him in those declining years.

CATHAL BRUGHA

"It's a strange coincidence that Tom Maguire died on the 71st anniversary of the fatal wounding of Cathal Brugha in O'Connell Street in Dublin and he is buried today, July 7, the day Cathal Brugha breathed his last in the Mater Hospital in Dublin.

"Tom would mention Brugha and his speech against the Treaty: 'If our last man was lying on the ground,' Brugha said, 'if our last shilling has been spent and our last cartridge fired and his enemies were howling around him, ready to plunge their bayonets into his body and if they should ask him, now will you come into our Empire, and he would say and he should say, true to the traditions that have gone before him, NO, and the British Empire and British rule in Ireland will have gone down for ever before that spirit dies out in Ireland'.

"A Thomáis, cuimhneoimid ort. You will live in our hearts and minds. You will live always. Long live the All-Ireland Republic and long live our Commandant General!" he concluded.

Dan Hoban called on piper Larry O'Dowd of Sligo to play one of the oldest Irish laments, Silent O' Moyle, which embraces the whole 32 Counties of Ireland, to conclude the ceremony. Larry O'Dowd was the piper who piped the martyred Mayo hunger-striker Michael Gaughan in 1974 all the way from the Isle of Wight to Leigue Cemetery in Ballina.

Among the attendance at the funeral was veteran Republican John Joe Hoey of New Jersey, USA who is a native of Kilmore, Co Roscommon. J. J. Hoey (82) was interned at the Curragh in the 1940s and was active in the Irish Freedom Committee in New York in the '50s and '60s. He remains active as an associate of George Harrison in New York.

Full military honours are rendered by an IRA firing party at the grave of General Maguire on January 21, 1994. (Above) the Volleys; (below) Present Arms

'STEADFAST, DETERMINED AND UPRIGHT... AN EXAMPLE OF COURAGE'

In an appreciation at the funeral Mass for Comdt General Maguire in Cross Church, Co Mayo on July 7, Dr Brian P. Murphy of Glenstal Abbey, Co Limerick paid tribute to the man and the great tradition which he embodies. Dr Murphy is a member of the Benedictine Community and author of *Patrick Pearse and the Lost Republican Ideal* (1991). As part of his research he conducted several interviews with Tom Maguire at his home in Mayo. We publish extracts from his address here:

"ONE IS very privileged to speak at the funeral of such a great and good man, Tom Maguire, on this historic occasion. One is also deeply aware of one's lack of qualification to speak. In particular I regret that I cannot address you in Irish, the language of his love — the language that his daughter-in-law, Pauline, told me he spoke most regularly at the end of his days.

Fortunately others have used the Irish language as the last rites were conducted in the family home and at the funeral Mass last night; and it will play a prominent part in today's ceremony. Tom Maguire would be happy to know that intercessions were made to the Lord on his behalf in the ancient language of this Ireland.

Our first duty is to commend the soul of Commandant General Thomas Maguire to the merciful care of God. While one can take consolation that a good man has gone to his rest and to his reward – has gone home as it were – we all have a sense of loss.

For his family there is the pain of losing a loved one, and for his friends there is a similar sadness and on this particular occasion an awareness that a great tradition has been broken.

TRADITION

Commandant General Tom Maguire was the last surviving member of the All-Ireland Republican Dáil Éireann of 1921. His passing is, therefore, a truly historic occasion. It might be claimed that he was also a most fitting survivor of the ideals of the Republican Dáil. He came from an ancient Irish lineage.

I recall asking him about his early family origins and he told me, as if it were yesterday, that his family had fought at the Battle of Aughrim, and it was after that they left Fermanagh and settled in the west. As he grew up in the west that became his family home he developed a love for the land, which he worked so well; for the language, which he spoke so affectionately; and for the Lord, whom he worshipped in the local Catholic Church.

A man of integrity he was related authentically to the ancient past of Ireland. It seems natural to apply to him the sentiments of Aodhgán Ó Rathaile uttered in his last days when, despairing that the old Gaelic order and ideals had been lost, he defiantly proclaimed that he would triumph in death:

I will stop from this on – death is near to me without delay, since the Chiefs of the Leamhan, Lein and Lee have been trodden underfoot. I will go under their protection into the cemetery with the 'Beloved One among the Heroes' – with those princes under whom my ancestors lived before Christ died.

Tom Maguire has joined those heroes of the past, but he has brought them a Christian dimension by making his 'Beloved One' Christ the Lord.

The events that give him title to be ranked among the heroes may be briefly recited: he was a member of the Irish Volunteers before the Easter Rising of 1916; in May 1921, despite being badly wounded, he led a successful ambush at Tourmakeady against British troops in the War of Independence; in that year he was elected to Dáil Éireann; he rejected the Treaty in January 1922; he was imprisoned in the Civil War and while in prison was told that his brother, Seán, had been shot as a reprisal victim; and he rejected De Valera's formation of Fianna Fáil in 1926 and the proposed entry into the Free State.

Until the end of his days he continued to oppose the recognition of a partitioned Ireland.

The historic sense is truly inspiring: it is hard to believe that we commit to the soil today a man who rubbed shoulders as an equal, as a Commandant General, with Collins, Brugha, De Valera and other leaders of the War of Independence some seventy-five years ago in the struggle for freedom.

I was vividly reminded of this historical significance a few years ago when, shortly after talking with Tom, I was reading the Lloyd George papers in the House of Lords Record Office. Contained in one of the files of documents there was an intelligence report for 30 September 1921, the period of the Truce, which stated that Tom Maguire had made a speech at Ballinrobe threatening that war would be renewed "if England tried to impose her will on Ireland".

When I reported my find to Tom he smiled and was intrigued to know that his name and his actions had come to the attention of Lloyd George in London during the preparations for the Treaty.

RECOGNITION

At that time Tom Maguire opposed the partition of Ireland, and over the last twenty-five years he has persistently opposed recognition by any nationalists of a partitioned country. Difficult decisions inevitably, and sadly, have led to divisions. Some have said of Tom that he lacked reality, that he was not pragmatic enough, that he was too intransigent.

Even his critics, however, have testified to his faithful fidelity to the Republican ideal. And as the litany of suffering and deaths continues more credibility is given to the simple statement of his life that partition was not the best way to reconcile the nationalist aspiration for unity with the unionist aspiration for Britishness. That Republican ideal had a distinguished pedigree and merits brief consideration.

Patrick Pearse gave expression to one aspect of the ideal in the poem *Renunciation* which was written just before Easter 1916:

> *I have turned my face*
> *To this road before me.*
> *To the deed that I see*
> *And the death I shall die.*

Thomas Maguire manifested the same dedication and commitment to the Republican oath and ideal as he walked the long hard road of life for over one hundred years.

Moreover, if the sentiments of Pearse fittingly convey the attitude of Tom Maguire, the qualities of Cathal Brugha tell us much about his own character. When I talked to Tom he praised Cathal Brugha because he was 'steadfast', 'determined', 'upright', and 'stood in the firing line'.

No greater tribute could be paid to Tom Maguire than to say that he lived according to the same ideals of Cathal Brugha: as a young man he was in the firing line; and at all times he was steadfast, determined and upright. One can discern in his faithful fidelity a touch of religious conviction and, in conclusion, it is fitting to return to the religious dimension of his death.

When I was asked to say this Mass I thought of a suitable text for the sermon. Immediately my mind was drawn to the feast day of St Thomas More and the readings for that Mass which were designed to convey the message of a man who died for a principle. The first reading was taken from the Old Testament Book of Maccabees.

It tells the story of Eleazar. A faithful Jew, he was ordered at the age of ninety years to eat pig's meat under pain of death. He resisted the threats of his enemies but the enticements of his friends were more difficult to overcome. They wanted him to live and encouraged him to pretend to eat pig's meat, while eating something else.

Keep the King happy they said by pretending to go through the ritual formula of eating pork; but in reality eat some other meat and tell your friends and followers later what you have done. I will leave you to see the full relevance with Tom Maguire.

NO DISSEMBLING

Suffice it to say that many times he was encouraged to pretend, to gloss over oaths and terms of treaties, but he always refused, there was no dissembling with him. He never had to explain or to excuse himself to his friends. The words of Eleazar may well be applied to him:

It does not suit with my time of life to play a part. Let me take leave of life with a good grace, as best suits my years, bequeathing to men younger than myself an example of courage.

That Tom Maguire has done. He has left an example of courage and merits the praise granted to good men in the Book of Ecclesiasticus:

Let us now praise famous men,
and our fathers that begat us.
What high achievement the Lord has made known in them,
ever since time began . . .
These men were the glories of their race,
the ornament of their time;
and the sons they begot have left a memory
that adds to the recital of their praise . . .
Their bodies lie in peace;
their name lasts on, age after age.
Their wisdom is yet a legend among the people;
wherever faithful men assemble
their story is told.

For the future we have a trust to be faithful to the memory of Tom Maguire; for the present we have a duty to pray for his soul. May he rest in peace. Amen"

MEDIA COVERAGE

With the exception of RTÉ, the national media carried the news of the death of Comdt-General Tom Maguire in some detail. Only the final RTÉ television news at 11.55pm on July 5 carried his passing, and then only briefly.

The Requiem Mass in Cross Church on July 7 was featured on the 6pm news that evening on RTÉ 1 television and the news in Irish at 6.55pm on Network 2 but was dropped from the main evening news at 9pm.

The national morning daily papers carried obituary notices on July 6-7 with the exception of the *Irish News* in Belfast which ignored it completely. The *Irish Post* in England (July 10) and the *Irish Echo* and *Irish Voice* (July 7) in the USA published obituaries and the *Sunday Tribune* carried a report of the funeral on July 11, as did *The Irish Times* in its July 8 edition.

Papers in the West of Ireland which paid tribute to him included the *Mayo News*, the *Connacht Telegraph*, the *Western People*, the *Tuam Herald*, the *Connaught Tribune* and the *Leitrim Observer*.

FEATURES

Raidió na Gaeltachta and Mid-West Radio had features on his passing while Liam Molloy of the *Tuam Herald* interviewed Nollaig Ó Gadhra about Comdt-General Maguire on Galway Bay FM.

Mayo Co Council voted sympathy and members paid tribute to his life work before adjourning their monthly meeting as a mark of respect on July 12. The Western Health Board passed a vote of sympathy at its July 5 meeting in Boyle, Co Roscommon.

The Grave of Rury, *by T. W. Rolleston (1857-1920) was read by Caoimhín Mac Cathmhaoil at Tom Maguire's funeral. Ruaidrí Ua Concubair, the last High King of Ireland, retired to Cong Abbey in 1186 A.D. and died and was buried there in 1198.*

"The far-off war of conquest" by the Anglo-Normans moved closer from the East as the High King, the symbol of All-Ireland sovereignty, lived out his declining years in Cong.

The reading of this poem was most appropriate as the last symbol of All-Ireland sovereignty 800 years later, Tom Maguire, lived out the last days of his life in Cross, a little over two miles from Cong Abbey, until he went to Castlebar in 1990 to be cared for by his devoted family.

THE GRAVE OF RURY

Clear as air, the western waters
Evermore their sweet, unchanging song
Murmur in their stony channels
Round O'Conor's sepulchre in Cong.

Crownless, hopeless, here he lingered;
Year on year went by him like a dream,
While the far-off roar of conquest
Murmured faintly like the singing stream.

Here he died, and here they tombed him,
Men of Fechin, chanting round his grave.
Did they know, ah! did they know it,
What they buried by the babbling wave?

Now above the sleep of Rury
Holy things and great have passed away;
Stone by stone the stately Abbey
Falls and fades in passionless decay.

Darkly grows the quiet ivy,
Pale the broken arches glimmer through;
Dark upon the cloister-garden
Dreams the shadow of the ancient yew.

Through the roofless aisles the verdure
Flows, the meadow-sweet and foxglove bloom.
Earth, the mother and consoler,
Winds soft arms about the lonely tomb.

Peace and holy gloom possess him,
Last of Gaelic monarchs of the Gael,
Slumbering by the young, eternal
River-voices of the western vale.

TRIBUTE FROM
GEORGE HARRISON, NEW YORK

The death of Comdt-General Tom Maguire took place on July 5, 1993 at age 101 in Castlebar, County Mayo, ending a life of uncompromising loyalty to the ideal of a free and independent Irish Republic; an Ireland totally free from all the shackles and tentacles of the monster octopus of British imperialism and its cancerous offsprings of sectarianism and puppet parliaments.

Much has been written of General Maguire since he passed on to join his old comrades in the Valhalla of Ireland's heroic dead. Those who have remained true to the legacy he has passed on will try to produce a memorial booklet dealing with the crucial issues he faced during his near century of struggle.

Starting out as a Volunteer in Cross, Co Mayo, he was appointed OC South Mayo Brigade and led the flying column in the Kilfall and Tourmakeady ambushes where he was seriously wounded.

He was later appointed to the rank of OC, 2nd Western Division, Irish Republican Army by Cathal Brugha, Minister for Defence at the time. He was then elected Sinn Féin TD for South Mayo. In 1921 he strongly opposed the treaty of surrender and when civil war broke out he became the leading loyal Republican figure in the west of Ireland and a member of the executive of the IRA.

He was captured in October 1922 by Free State forces and interned in Athlone. General Maguire was one of six men set aside for execution in January 1923... five of them died before Free State firing squads.

In April 1923 his younger brother Seán, a mere youth of 17 years, was executed with five others in Tuam Workhouse. The firing squads were busy... This was one of the dirtiest of their many acts of infamy.

General Maguire escaped from Athlone in June 1923 and was never recaptured. He remained staunch and true to the ideals and principles he espoused in his youth and which led his brother and many of his comrades to early graves. To some of us who grew up in Mayo and followed him into the arena of anti-imperialist struggle he was a legend and an almost god-like figure.

In 1938 General Maguire and the surviving faithful members of the Second Dáil Éireann delegated authority to the Army Council of the IRA. And in December 1969, during an internal crisis in the Irish Republican Movement, he recognised the Provisional IRA as the legitimate successor to the 1938 body.

He journeyed to the United States more than once and reaffirmed his unwavering commitment to the ideal of his youth. In 1976 his fellow Mayoman Frank Stagg died while on hunger strike in an English dungeon and his mortal remains were seized by Free State forces in a cowardly and obscene act of state brutality.

General Maguire delivered the eulogy at his symbolic funeral in February 1976. During yet another critical internal conflict in the Irish Republican Movement, General Maguire disagreed with the IRA decision to support Sinn Féin taking seats and to enter Leinster House. He issued the following statement which speaks for itself:

"There is no difference between entering the partition parliament of Leinster House and entering a partition parliament of Stormont.

"I speak as the sole surviving Teachta Dála of the Second Dáil Éireann and as the sole surviving member of the Executive of the Second Dáil Éireann.

"In December 1969, as the sole surviving member of the Executive of the Second Dáil Éireann, I recognised the Provisional Army Council, which remained true to the Irish Republic as the lawful Army of the Thirty-two County Irish Republic.

"I do not recognise the legitimacy of any Army Council styling itself the Council of the Irish Republican Army which lends support to any person or organisation styling itself as Sinn Féin and prepared to enter the partition parliament, and in doing so broke faith and betrayed the trust placed in their predecessors in 1969.

"The Irish Republic, proclaimed in arms in Easter Week 1916 and established by the democratic majority vote of the people in the general election of 1918, has been defended by Irish Republicans for several generations. Many have laid down their lives in that defence. Many others have suffered imprisonment and torture. I am confident that the Cause so nobly served will yet triumph.

"Dated the 22 day of October, 1986."

Tom Maguire was the last survivor of the Second Dáil and the last person to hold the rank of Comdt-General in the Irish Republican Army. He was patron of Sinn Féin Poblachtach and took a keen interest in the organisation right up to his death.

At a suitable time General Maguire will be remembered in this city. May the green sod of his native Mayo rest lightly over him and may his heroic and unconquered spirit rest in eternal peace.

To all his family deep condolence.

Respectfully,
— George Harrison
Brooklyn, New York

80 Ans Au Service De La Liberté

Tom Maguire est décédé le 5 juillet 1993

Dernière personne vivante à porter le titre de 'Commandant général de l'Armée républicaine irlandaise', Tom Maguire est décédé à Castlebar à l'âge de 101 ans (1892-1993).

Parrain de Sinn Féin Poblachtach depuis 1987, il était aussi le dernier représentant vivant du second 'Dáil Éireann', où il avait été élu en 1921.

(Dáil Éireann: Parlement de l'Irlande réunifiée, unie).

Ayant rejoint lesá 'Irish volunteers' dès leur création en 1913, il dirigea la brigade de Mayo de l'I.R.A. avant d'être le commandant de la 'Brigade Flying Column'.

Plusieurs fois capturé et évadé, il devint Vice-président de Sinn Féin en 1931.

Dans la grande tradition du Dáil (All-Ireland Parliament), avec les survivants du premier parlement irlandais, il délégua l'autorité exécutive au Conseil de l'Armée de l'I.R.A. en 1938.

En 1969, il reconnaissait le 'Provisional Army Council' comme le successeur légitime de celui de 1938.

Considérant comme toujours valable le Parlement des 32 Comtés voté en 1921, il refusa de reconnaître l'autorité du Parlement des 26 comtés et devint parrain de S. F. Poblachtach en 1987; suivant en celà la ligne préconisée par Ruairí Ó Brádaigh, et considérant que la ligne suivie par Sinn Féin sous la direction de Gerry Adams reconnaissait 'de fait' le Parlement des 26 comtés.

En 1986 il écrivait: 'Je ne reconnais la légitimité d'aucun Conseil de l'Armée repésentant le Conseil de l'Armée Républicaine irlandaise qui apporterait son soutien à toute personne ou organisation représentant Sinn Féin se préparant à entériner la partition du Parlement de Leinster House'.

Pour l'anniversaire de ses 100 ans il avait reçu des télégrammes du monde entier.

Tom Maguire a été inhumé au cimetière de Castlebar le 7 juillet 1993, son cercueil drapé dans une bannière spéciale portant les anciens insignes de l'I.R.A. et la mention 'Arm Phoblacht na hÉireann' (Armée du Peuple d'Irlande).

Il rejoint ainsi les autres grands noms de l'histoire moderne du républicanisme irlandais, Collins, Brugha, de Valera et tous les dirigeants de la guerre d'indépendance dans leur combat pour la liberté.

C.C.

Report in Emgann/Combat Breton no. 94, 1993

De Generaal Is Dood

Old soldiers never die zeggen ze wel eens, maar dat heeft niet kunnen voorkomen dat op 5 juli het laatst overgebleven lid van de historische tweede Dáil de laatste adem uitblies. Tom Maguire, de laatste nog levende generaal van het Irish Republican Army, werd 101jaar en bleef tot zijn laatste snik een overtuigde en compromisloze republikein. In hart en nieren een vechtersbaas moest hij niets hebben van de valse beloften van politici en collaborateurs. Daarom werd hij in 1986 lid van Republican Sinn Féin.

In 1913 sloot hij zich aan bij de Irish Volunteers en in 1919 werd hij commandant van de South Mayo brigade. In mei 1921 werd hij in het Ierse parlement gekozen en in datzelfde jaar werd hij benoemd tot algemeen bevelhebber van de Tweede Westelijke divisie van het republikeinse leger. In die hoedanigheid volvoerde hij een aantal huzarenstukjes in gevechten met het Britse leger. Hij verwierp het verdrag dat tot de deling van Ierland leidde en werd geïnterneerd door de overheid van de Vrijstaat. Hij ontkwam ternauwernood aan executie en ontsnapte in 1923 uit gevangenschap en werd nooit meer opgespoord. Bij de verkiezingen in datzelfde jaar werd hij in het illegale heel Ierland vertegenwoordigende parlement gekozen. Omdat hij weigerde de eed van trouw aan de Britse koning af te leggen kon hij geen kandidaat meer staan in de daaropvolgende verkiezingen. In 1969 erkende hij de Provisional Army Council als de legitieme opvolger van het vooroorlogse republikeinse leger.

– Report in *Ierland Bulletin*, Netherlands

IRISH POST AUGUST 7, 1993

Australian Commemoration

Commandant General Tom Maguire, the last survivor of the second Dáil Eireann who died in early July, has been commemorated by Australia's Irish community at a Sydney ceremony. A book of condolences has also been opened by the Irish National Association, Sydney's main Irish body. Among those attending the Sydney ceremony was 92-year-old Cyril Carroll, who joined the IRA in 1917 and served in the second and sixth Dublin brigades. He later fought for the Républicans as adjutant to the Second Eastern Division before emigrating to Australia in 1924.

Mort du Commandant Général
Tom Maguire
1892-1993

Il avait rejoint les Irish Volunteers à leur création en 1913. En 1919, il commandait la brigade de l'IRA de South Mayo et sa 'Flying Column' (motorisée).

Il prit part à de nombreux combats. Son unité encerclée par 600 britanniques, ayant été blessé 6 fois il réussit à briser l'encerclement. En 1921, il devenait député Sinn Féin de South Mayo-South Roscommon. Puis nommé général de la 2e Division de l'Ouest, il dut affronter la guerre civile car il rejeta le traité de 1921. Il fut nommé membre du QG de l'IRA qui en 1922 rejeta le traité.

Un Héros Légendaire

Il fut alors capturé par les forces de l'Etat Libre en octobre 1922 et interné. En janvier 1923 il était promis au poteau d'exécution avec 5 autres républicains. Il put s'évader et ne fut jamais repris. Il fut de nouveau élu en 1923. En 1927, il ne prit pas part aux élections, car les républicains ne reconnaissaient pas l'Etat Libre, soumis au roi d'Angleterre (l'Irlande ne devint République qu'en 1948).

Un Républicain sans Concession

En 1931, il fut élu vice-président du Sinn Féin et en 1938, avec les survivants du 2e Dáil, il vota la délégation de l'autorité dans la lutte au conseil de l'IRA (décision toujours en vigueur pour les républicains). En 1969, il reconnut l'IRA provisoire comme légitime successeur de l'IRA. En 1986, il a soutenu ceux qui ont quitté Sinn Féin pour fonder Republican Sinn Féin avec Ruairí Ó Brádaigh.

Solidarité Irlande salue la mémoire de ce grand combattant pour une Irlande Libre de 32 comtés.

– Report in *Solidarité Irlande*
No. 9, 1993, Brest

Ballad of Tourmakeady Fight

*(Carried out by South Mayo Flying Column,
under Comdt-General Tom Maguire, on May 3, 1921;
composed by Mr Huets, Tourmakeady)*

Along the Partry Mountains, we had a dreadful day;
In war we were surrounded, all on the third of May.
My mind it was completely gone, it seemed to me a dream,
When bullets flew like hailstones at Bealanidaun stream.

At Tholly-ard and Loregan, they're now on the record,
Our heroes won the battlefield, all praises to the Lord,
They fought like loyal Irishmen along the mountainside –
May God be with them everywhere, and always be their guide.

The bullets they were whizzing 'round, and flying like the hail –
I often heard, "Success attend the sons of Granuaile!"
They drove away the enemy, in terror they did go;
It yields a lot of credit to the County of Mayo.

Upon the sides of Loregan, the Volunteers did say,
"Cheer up my gallant Irishmen, we now have won the day.
The soldiers we have conquered on the slopes of Roy-an-ore,
God is with us 'on the run' and will for evermore!"

A party of these soldiers came down by Loughan Shee,
Their ranks were badly broken, and down they had to flee;
They joined in conversation, saying, "Now we've got our fill
Of all the Partry Mountains – they're worse than Vinegar Hill!"

It's now we join in chorus, and thank the Lord on High,
Who saved our brave Sinn Féiners when danger it was nigh;
They proved themselves St Patrick's sons, no danger did they fear –
Long live the Tourmakeady boys and the Irish Volunteers!

The Volunteers were everywhere successful on that day,
Except for poor O'Brien, who fell all in the fray;
He died for dear old Ireland, the bravest of the brave,
May the Lord have mercy on his soul; he now lies in the grave.

Man-of-Oak Maguire

in Cong
sprouted the strong sapling
nurtured by the sacred fossils
of Gaelic High Kings
whispered to by patriots
from Emmet to Pearse
unbending with any breeze
man-of-oak
Maguire.

Stood
by the Republic
by the oath of Fenians
by young Irelands dream
by the creed of Tone
for him no stepping stone
but the green branch blooming
from the northern shores of Derry
to the Kingdom of Kerry
man-of-oak
Maguire

unfelled
rising proud neath western skies
for over 100 years
of wounding bloody spears
from foreign invaders
and those who did their bidding
lesser twigs who "took the shilling"
could not barter
man-of-oak
Maguire.

all along
the gentle grassy slopes of Cong
bitter the lament of the Banshee
unheard since the death of Ard Rí
Achone! Achone! Achone!
Man-of-oak
Maguire
is gone.

Seán Hallinan
Claremorris
July 1993